Solomon's
SONG OF SONGS
and Issues of Love & Sex

Dirk Waren

Soaring Eagle Press

Solomon's SONG OF SONGS and Issues of Love & Sex

Other translations are listed in the Bibliography.

All underlining, italics and bracketed notes in scriptural quotes are added by the author.

Pronominal references to Deity in this work are not always capitalized.

Edited by KEEII with special thanks to Raquel J. for motivation.

Cover photo (at Lake Erie, OH) and back cover photo (at Buhl Park, PA) by Jennifer Waren.

ISBN: 979-8-218-04157-1
PUBLISHED BY SOARING EAGLE PRESS
Youngstown

Printed in the United States of America

…for love is as strong as death,
its jealousy unyielding as the grave.
It burns like blazing fire,
like a mighty flame.

- Song of Songs 8:6

CONTENTS

Introduction

About this Book

This work examines Solomon's Song of Songs — the most controversial book of the Bible — and its themes of romantic love, marriage and sex. As such, it honestly addresses several interesting topics: some beautiful, some noble, some private and some potentially awkward.

Obviously we're going to look at some adult-oriented issues so those who can't stomach this kind of frank subject matter, for whatever reason, are encouraged to hold off for now.

PART I

Solomon's Song of Songs

This part focuses on the Song of Songs itself, providing general information on this poetic book of the Bible, as well as offering the top interpretations and key insights that'll bless your walk with the Lord and your life in general, particularly in areas of romantic love, marriage and sex.

We'll also look at forms of art in the Scriptures since the Song of Songs is a Holy Spirit-inspired work of art.

1

General Q&A on the Song of Songs

This chapter answers myriad key questions concerning this distinctive piece of God's Word by mining it for insights, along with related resources. Whenever an answer is uncertain, the best possible ones are supplied.

What Is the Song of Songs?

The Song of Songs is a poetic book of the Hebraic Scriptures — the Old Testament — that consists of the lyrics to a love song in eight chapters. It follows the books of Proverbs and Ecclesiastes; and precedes the prophetic books, which begin with Isaiah.

The Song of Songs is relatively short at eight chapters in poetic verse and can be cursorily read in about 20 minutes.

The fact that there are multiple speaking parts, including choruses of people, suggest that it was acted out as a musical, possibly as part of a week-long wedding festival (e.g. Genesis 29:27-28). Keep in mind that poetry, songs and stories were entertainment in ancient times, just as concerts, movies and shows are to us today.

Who Wrote the Song of Songs?

The very first verse plainly states: "Solomon's Song of Songs" with the literal Hebrew reading "The Song of Songs that [is] of Solomon," thus it was written by Solomon. This corresponds to the fact that Solomon "spoke three thousand proverbs and **his songs numbered a thousand and five**" (1 Kings 4:32).

This incidentally explains why the book is often listed in some translations as the Song of Solomon, as it is in the King James Version and New King James Version.

When Was It Written?

Since the cities noted in the song involve both northern and southern Israel, the events of the story and the time of composition indicate any time during Solomon's reign from 971-931 BC, which was before the kingdom was divided into Israel (north) and Judah (south) after Solomon's rule (1 Kings 11:41-12:33).

Why Is It Called the "Song of Songs"?

Of the 1005 songs that Solomon wrote this was obviously his greatest song, his 'magnum opus,' and no doubt his longest. Thus he dubbed it accordingly, inspired by the Holy Spirit (2 Peter 1:21). It literally means the "best of songs." Similar wording can be observed in other biblical phrases like Lord of Lords, King of

Kings, and Holy of Holies. You could say it was Solomon's "greatest hit" or "triple-platinum record."

Is It an Anthology of Love Poems?

The reality that the Song of Songs is Solomon's *greatest* song and that it's "God-breathed," as is all Scripture (2 Timothy 3:16), rules out the theory of modern scholars that it is simply an ancient collection of secular love poems from Mesopotamia, Egypt and Greece. This "anthology" interpretation is also invalidated by the glaring literary unity of the song, as observed by repeated phrases and ideas, such as "the daughters of Jerusalem/Zion" (1:5, 2:7, 3:5, 3:10-11, 5:8, 5:16 & 8:4).

The fact that this book of the Bible is an epic **love song** explains the challenge of discerning a coherent story. The nature of song lyrics & poetry is to convey emotions and spur intrigue, images, ideas and morals above a point-by-point saga. As art, the Song of Songs inspires people one way or another and is written in such a way to leave room for interpretation.

A couple of good modern examples would be songs like *The Sound of Silence* and *Stairway to Heaven*. Has anyone yet been able to conclusively figure out what these classic songs are about or what they mean? Ask ten different people and you'll get ten different answers. That's part of the appeal of art appreciation — putting the pieces of the puzzle together, finding the meaning(s), gleaning from the art and allowing it to enhance your life one way or another.

That's what the Song of Songs is all about with the obvious distinction that it's not just human art, but also Holy Spirit-inspired Scripture.

Why Has It Been Considered "Controversial" by Some?

Because it's a love song filled with overtly romantic statements between lovers, including references to potential sex or desired sex (e.g. Song of Songs 7:6-9), as well as other passionate proclamations (e.g. 2:3-6).

Those who have questioned the book's inclusion in the biblical canon obviously felt that human romance/sexuality is an inappropriate topic for Holy Scripture. Yet isn't romantic love and everything that goes with it a significant part of life on this Earth? Wouldn't the very Creator of men, women and sex have something helpful to say on such a relevant topic in God's instruction manual for humanity?

We have to remember in these days of gross sexual immorality that sex itself is *not* evil; it's sexual *immorality* that is evil. The LORD created sex while the devil — "the god of this world" (2 Corinthians 4:4) — perverts it.

How Was the Song of Songs Determined to be Part of the Canon of Scripture?

From earliest times the book formed a part of the Hebrew canon of Scripture and was read annually at Passover.

However, due to its supposedly controversial content, the Song of Songs place in the Hebraic canon was still debated as late as 90 AD at the Council of Jamnia where it was affirmed by Jewish rabbis, including Akiva.

Should the Book Be Taken at Face Value as a Love Story or as an Allegory?

Since the LORD's relationship with Israel is depicted as a marriage (Isaiah 50:1, Jeremiah 2:2, Ezekiel 23 & Hosea 2:2) and the Church is the "bride of Christ" (2 Corinthians 11:2 & Revelation 19:7-9), the Song of Songs *could* be taken in an allegorical sense of God's Love for Israel or Christ's love for his Church. I've heard a couple of effective sermons by Mike Bickle that interpreted the book this way.

However, the traditional idea from hymnology that Christ is the "rose of Sharon" or "lily of the valleys" based on Song of Songs 2:1 is erroneous since the woman in the story is speaking, not the man. Meanwhile there are issues that arise when interpreting the book in a strictly allegorical sense; for instance, the image of Christ resting between the breasts of the Church based on 1:13. The motivation for this exclusively allegorical interpretation seems rooted in embarrassment over the explicit erotic references.

As such, the Song of Songs should first and foremost be taken as an amazing love story between a biological man and biological woman with numerous lessons on romantic love and marriage, many of which are covered in chapters **4** and **5**.

You could sum up the book like so: God made romantic attraction and the marital covenant for the husband & wife's enjoyment and this love can be viewed as a picture of the Lord's joy in his people.

Where Do the Events of the Song Take Place?

The love story combines rural and urban locations. Jerusalem is the city where Solomon's palace was located while the rural areas would be the hill country north of Jerusalem where Solomon's vineyards, herds and flocks were located, not to mention where the maiden hailed from in Shunem.

How Long Do the Events Entail?

Assuming it's a chronological account without gaps, the story occurs over the course of a year and some weeks/months, but no more than two years. This is based on the first spring being mentioned in Song of Songs 2:11-13 and the second spring near the end of the book in 7:12.

Who is the Woman in the Story?

Since she is referred to as a Shulammite in Song of Songs 6:13,[1] she was a maiden from Shunem, which was/is a village located 3 miles north of Jezreel in southern Galilee, roughly 55 miles north of Jerusalem. (Shulem and Shunem are synonymous, by the way, as observed by 1 Kings 1:3, 2 Kings 4:8 and Joshua 19:18). This disqualifies the theory that she was Pharaoh's daughter, one of Solomon's early wives, as detailed in 1 Kings 3:1.

While Shunem is about 30 miles south of the border of Lebanon, it's squarely in Israel. I point this out because I've heard one or two commentators refer to the maiden as Lebanese, likely because the land of Lebanon is mentioned seven times in the song (e.g. 4:8). However, the text plainly calls her a "Shulammite," aka an Israelite from the village of Shunem, which — again — is just 55 miles north of the capitol city.

---

[1] Some translations spell Shulammite with one 'm' and hence Shulamite, such as the KJV and NKJV. In this book we'll go with the more widespread Shulammite.

Since she was a Shulammite, some favor the idea that she was Abishag *(ab-ee-SHAG)*, the virgin who was enlisted to take care of the elderly King David and keep him warm in bed without having sexual relations (1 Kings 1:1-4,15). The fact that the Bible describes Abishag as "very beautiful" in 1 Kings 1:4 corresponds to the description of the maiden in Song of Songs as flawless and the "most beautiful of women" (1:8, 4:7 & 6:1). However, the fact that Solomon neglected to call her Abishag in the Song of Songs and failed to mention how she cared for his elderly father — and this was, in fact, how he met her — pretty much cancels out this theory.

I've read one or two commentaries where the author refers to the maiden by the name Shulamith, obviously based on the fact that she's called a Shulammite in 6:13. This is odd since the term identifies where she's from, not her personal name. It'd be like calling me Meccanite because I hail from Mecca, Ohio.

This leaves us with the woman simply being an unnamed maiden from Shunem whose family was possibly employed by King Solomon in the hill country north of Jerusalem wherein he had vineyards, as wells as herds and flocks (Song of Songs 8:11 & Ecclesiastes 2:4-7). It's even more likely that her family owned vineyards/animals near Solomon's fields.

A further consideration is that the Shulammite woman is simply a character in a fictional love story that Solomon was inspired by the Holy Spirit to write, sort of like an ancient-epic spiritual version of John Cougar Mellencamp's ditty about Jack & Diane.

Who is the Man in the Love Story?

Solomon is the knee-jerk answer since the king is referred to numerous times in the book (1:1, 1:5, 3:7, 3:9, 3:11, 8:11 & 8:12), but there's also a shepherd lover who isn't likely the king of Israel, although he arguably could be (1:7). It depends on what interpretation one embraces, which brings up…

2

The Five Main Interpretations of the Story

There are several interpretations of the Song of Songs because it's not always clear who's speaking in any given verse or verses. Most versions of the Bible add headings to identify who is speaking in order to help readers understand the story. But these headings are *not* part of the original text; they were added by the translators of the version in question. This explains why the King James Version doesn't include headings.

Here are the five chief interpretations:

Interpretation #1: A Historical Account of Solomon and His First Love

According to this reading, Solomon meets the young woman from Shunem when he's visiting his vineyards north of Jerusalem and is profoundly smitten by her. She is Solomon's first true love and becomes his first wife.

In his older, more experienced years Solomon advocated one wife in Ecclesiastes 9:9, and I'm sure (assuming this interpretation is the correct one) that he intended for this nubile woman from the country to be his one-and-only.

But, as noted in the previous chapter, the events in the Song of Songs only cover a year and some weeks/months; Solomon ludicrously went on to marry hundreds of foreign women for political reasons, as he did with Pharaoh's daughter, which the LORD had instructed his people *not* to do (1 Kings 3:1, 11:1-4, Deuteronomy 17:17 & Exodus 34:15-16). In other words, Solomon sinned by marrying these myriad foreign wives. Not only did they take his attention away from his first love (the Shulammite maiden), even worse, they led him astray from pure devotion to the LORD and into idolatry.

So, this particular view of the Song of Songs depicts Solomon's relationship with his first love *before* he transgressed by marrying multiple foreign women, which brought about his downfall. If this reading is true, obviously God thinks this relationship in its short context is a fitting example from which to learn about romance, love and marriage *despite* Solomon's ensuing moral failure in the years to come.

Let me offer a real-life example to defend this position (even though I personally don't favor it): I worked with a guy for several years three decades ago who was the best possible worker you could imagine. He was exceptional, but went on to work for another company in the same basic position. As the years progressed, he grew weary of his occupation and started to engage in unethical practices even though he still "got the job done." For instance, he'd be on the clock while not present at work. I'd have no problem citing this man as a prime example of the ideal worker when he was younger, but not in his later years. The same principle applies to the Solomon depicted in the Song of Songs vs. the polygamous, idolatrous Solomon of 1 Kings 11:1-4 or the disillusioned Solomon of Ecclesiastes.

For those who object to Solomon being the sole male lover in the Song of Songs on the grounds that the king of Israel would be too busy with royal duties and would not have time for lowly activities like shepherding flocks (1:7), we know from other passages that King Solomon had vineyards in the hill country north of Jerusalem, as wells as herds and flocks (Song of Songs 8:11 & Ecclesiastes 2:4-7). Would he not get "out" and personally check on them from time to time? In regards to shepherding flocks, isn't it possible that his father, David, informed him about how instrumental shepherding sheep was to becoming an effective, noble leader of God's people (2 Samuel 7:8)?

Thus young Solomon would get away from the hubbub of political big city life and spend a few nights here or there in retreat, overseeing his herds and flocks. This would cultivate intimacy with the LORD, especially at night under the quiet starry panorama, as well as keep him in touch with the common people of Israel. I'm in fulltime ministry and I regularly take the time to go primitive camping or hiking, gazing at the stars at night seeking the LORD.

The basic outline for this interpretation is as follows (based on John MacArthur's take):

I. The Wooing: "Leaving" (1:2-3:5)
  A. The Couple's Reminiscences (1:2-2:7)
  B. The Couple's Expression of Mutual Love (2:8-3:5)
II. The Marriage Ceremony: "Cleaving" (3:6-5:1)
  A. The Regal Bridegroom (3:6-11)
  B. The Wedding and Consummation (4:1-5:1a)
  C. The LORD's Approval (5:1b)
III. The Marital Covenant: "Weaving" (5:2-8:14)
  A. The Initial Disagreement (5:2-6:3)
  B. The Mending (6:4-8:4)
  C. Developing in Grace (8:5-14)

Here's another one, a simpler variation by Don Anderson:

I. Courtship (1:1-2:17)
II. Commitment (3:1-5:1)
III. Challenge (5:2-6:13)
IV. Communion (7:1-8:14)

Interpretation #2: A Historical Account of Solomon when He Already Had 60 Wives and 80 Concubines

This position is the same as above except that King Solomon already has 60 wives and 80 concubines by the time he meets the Shulammite maiden. Here's the passage that supports this reading wherein the king is (presumably) speaking:

> **8 Sixty queens there may be,**
> **and eighty concubines,**
> **and virgins beyond number;**
> **9 but my dove, my perfect one, is unique,**

the only daughter of her mother,
the favorite of the one who bore her.
The young women saw her and called her blessed;
the queens and concubines praised her.
Song of Songs 6:8-9

The obvious problem with this interpretation is that the Shulammite maiden is clearly head-over-heals in love with her beloved, but would she be this excited if she knew she had to share him with no less than 140 women, not to mention the likelihood of hundreds more in the years to come? (As noted earlier, Solomon's harem eventually grew to 700 wives and 300 concubines, as evidenced in 1 Kings 11:3).

Then there's additional problem of the Shulammite's repeated statement that "**My beloved <u>is mine</u>**" (2:16 & 6:3). *If* Solomon had 60 other wives at this time he'd also be the possession of these myriad other spouses (to say nothing of his 80 concubines), which of course makes such a statement wholly untrue.

Do the math: If Solomon acquired 700 wives during his 40-year reign, which is 480 months (or 2080 weeks), that means there'd be on average a wedding festival at the palace about every 3 weeks! Keep in mind that these wedding feasts would last *days*, even up to a week or more (see Jesus' Parable of the Wedding Banquet in Matthew 22:1-14). Imagine being Solomon's wife and having to celebrate your husband marrying a new spouse that often! Even if you were his 'favorite' — his "queen of queens"— you definitely *couldn't* call him "yours." He'd be "yours" only in an extremely fractional sense.

In light of these glaring issues, the man is likely just describing the woman from Shunem as "one in a million" when distinguishing her from "sixty queens," "eighty concubines" and "virgins beyond number." The male lover basically says as much in 2:2 with his words "Like a lily among thorns is my darling among the young women."

This corresponds to his exaggerated statement that there was "no flaw" in her (4:7); and is also supported by the fact that Solomon doesn't include any language in his song about ownership or relationship with these "sixty queens," "eighty concubines" and "virgins beyond number." Furthermore, the numerical progression from sixty to eighty to "beyond number" points to poetic hyperbole — exaggeration for effect — rather than literalism.

Interpretation #3: Solomon Wrote the Song as a Largely Fictional Love Story Involving a Monogamous Version of Himself

In this reading the love story is fictional, a work of art, albeit spiced with elements from Solomon's real-life experiences, much as modern writers and composers create stories/lyrics with bits taken from real life, such as the characters in the tale. As these writers have a message to convey with their art, so did Solomon, albeit he was inspired by the Holy Spirit (2 Peter 1:21 & 2 Timothy 3:16).

For those who have an issue with Solomon using an idealized version of himself as the male protagonist in the story, artists do this all the time in their works. For instance, M. Night Shyamalan cast himself as an author in his movie *Lady in the Water* whose writings would be the seed to changing the world (while I didn't have a problem with this, some critics understandably knocked Shyamalan for being pretentious).

Another example is William Shatner. When asked how he approached the iconic character of Captain Kirk on Star Trek, he said he simply played himself, just a more heroic version. Likewise, Solomon is playing himself in this epic love song, just an idealized version.

No one knows the exact date that Solomon wrote the Song of Songs in the 10th century BC but, assuming he wrote it in his later years (and assuming this interpretation is valid), he would've regretted his moral failures concerning his vast harem & idolatries and so wrote this magnum opus to, in effect, right those wrongs by offering a positive message to the public concerning romantic love & marriage and everything that goes with it.

Think about it like this, have you ever shared a story from your past, but downplayed your flaws and transgressions? Most of us have. Even the Bible itself does this concerning King David: When 1 Chronicles 20:1-3 details the era in David's reign involving his adultery with Bathsheba and murder of her husband (detailed in 2 Samuel 11:1–12:23), it omits these transgressions altogether, choosing instead to focus on David's victories over the Ammonites.

Why would Chronicles leave out this notable bit of infamy? Because the historical books of Samuel & Kings focused on telling the good, the bad and the ugly of Israel, which informed the Hebrews how they ended up in exile. Chronicles, by contrast, was originally written to the Jews returning to the Promised Land after 70 years of exile who wanted to know if they still fit into God's plan. In other words, they didn't *need* to dwell on the sordid details of their national history at that particular time. They needed to be encouraged about their national identity and history, not made ashamed and deflated.

Interpretation #4: A Commoner Becomes "King for the Day" at His Wedding Feast

In this interpretation the male is not really Solomon, but rather a commoner who is entertained for a week, along with his bride, as "king and queen" during their wedding feast (e.g. Genesis 29:27-28). In short, the two lovers are engaging in fantasy, using imagery of royalty to reflect their affection for one another.

The reasoning behind this reading is twofold: Solomon would've been too busy with his national duties to have time for a pastoral romance, not to mention the man in the love story is depicted as a shepherd in 1:7 and it's difficult to imagine the king of Israel spending his time tending sheep. This perspective also resolves the conundrum of God using Solomon — who notoriously had 700 wives and 300 concubines during his reign — as the key character in a biblical book conveying truths on ideal love and marriage.

The problem with this explanation is that it's just too vague and fails to explain the distinct references to King Solomon, his carriage, his 60-warrior escorts, Jerusalem and so forth.

Interpretation #5: A Love Triangle Involving Solomon, the Shulammite and Her Beloved Shepherd

In this reading there are three characters in the love story wherein King Solomon falls in love with the beautiful Shulammite maiden upon meeting her while visiting his vineyards north of Jerusalem. He whisks her away to his palace in the big city hoping to win her heart so that she'll be his queen of queens, but she only has eyes for a young shepherd from her own community to whom she has been promised. She proves herself faithful to him and so Solomon eventually releases her to marry the shepherd with his sanction and that of her family.

While this narrative requires the reader to disregard many of the typical headings *added* to the text by well-meaning translators (which are not Scripture) and read-in-between-the-lines, it resolves several problematic points:

1. The issue of the king of Israel being depicted as a lowly shepherd (1:7, 2:16 & 6:2-3) by insisting that there are *two* male protagonists — King Solomon *and* a young shepherd.
2. The issue of the LORD dubiously using polygamous Solomon for biblical lessons on romantic love and marriage.
3. The issue of the "daughters of Jerusalem" requiring a description of the man the Shulammite maiden loves (5:9-6:3), which makes no sense if the man is King Solomon since they'd already be well familiar with the top celebrity of Israel.
4. The issue of the guardsmen of the city not seeming to know that the Shulammite lass is their boss' desired woman or vice versa (3:1-4 & 5:2-7). It's true that the first sequence *might* be a dream and the second one definitely is a nightmare wherein the watchmen beat her up and steal her cloak, but would King Solomon likely write in his greatest song such a fantasy tale of gross insubordination against the king of Israel? In other words, the more fitting interpretation is that the lover whom she was searching for was not King Solomon, the boss of the watchmen, but rather some nondescript shepherd from the sticks up north.

We'll look at this "three-character view" further in chapter **5**.

3

Additional Q&A

Let's consider a few extra questions about the Song of Songs not covered in chapter **1**.

Who Are the Peripheral Characters in the Story?

While Solomon and the Shulammite maiden are the dominant characters in the story, and also perhaps her betrothed lover (*if* the "shepherd hypothesis" is valid), there are some minor characters with speaking parts as follows:

- The "daughters of Jerusalem" (1:4, 1:11, 5:8-9 & 5:16-6:1), which are young ladies from the city, and likely virgins since the Shulammite repeatedly charges them to not awaken love until it so desires (e.g. 2:7).
- The citizens of the city (3:6-11).
- The friends of the male protagonist (6:13).
- A relative (8:5).
- The maiden's brothers (2:15 & 8:8-9).
- Also, the LORD is possibly speaking in 5:1 (more on this momentarily).

Again, the headings supplied in many English Bibles, which delineate the character or characters speaking, are not included in the original Hebrew text. This explains why the King James Version omits such headings. These headings are educated guesses by the translators of the version in question.

Most of the above characters and corresponding citation links are from the NKJV. Meanwhile the NIV simply refers to all of the peripheral characters as “friends” without specifying their identity further.

Why is God Not Mentioned in the Song of Songs?

Because the LORD doesn’t *have* to be mentioned in a love song. God isn’t directly referenced in the book of Esther either. Yet this doesn’t mean the Creator is utterly absent from these biblical books as “All Scripture is God-breathed” (2 Timothy 3:16) and the Almighty works in the lives of people to fulfill Divine will, as it is written: “for it is God who works in you to will and to act in order to fulfill his good purpose” (Philippians 2:13).

Martin Luther put it like this: “God himself will milk the cows through him whose vocation that is. He who engages in the lowliness of his work performs God’s work.”

Thus in Esther we see the LORD working *through* the titular woman and Mordecai, not to mention ordinary people, to deliver the Hebrews exiled in Persia from a satanic plot of genocide. On a much more pleasant note, in the Song of Songs God is involved behind the scenes in the loving relationship of the Shulammite maiden and the shepherd lover (regardless of whether or not the shepherd is a nondescript young Hebrew or the king of Israel).

How do we know this beyond the Song of Songs being a part of the Hebraic Scriptures? Because the events take place in Israel at the height of its united kingdom after the righteous reign of David, "a man after God's own heart" (Acts 13:22). As such, both the Shulammite maiden and the shepherd would've sought the LORD about something as important as a lifelong mate and God arranged their meeting behind the scenes (we'll look at this notion further in the next chapter in the section on arranged marriages).

This offers a lesson for believers: Not every work of art we create or every story we tell or every service we provide has to explicitly mention the Lord in order to effectively bless people. Often the subtle approach is the route to take rather than smashing people over the head with overt Christian verbiage.

Lastly, as noted in the previous section, God *is* included in the Song of Songs since the Creator is presumably the one speaking as the couple consummates their marriage:

> **"Eat, friends, and drink;**
> **drink your fill of love."**
>
> **Song of Songs 5:1c**

Since it would be inappropriate for friends & relatives of the couple to eavesdrop on their lovemaking — whether then or now — this is evidently a reference to the LORD blessing their wonderful union.

We have to get away from this Victorian myth that our Creator is prudish. God invented male and female human beings and their sex organs. In other words, he created the very idea of romantic attraction, marriage and sex.

The LORD's attitude toward the couple's relationship and union brings to mind this passage:

> [18]**Three things cause wonder for me;**
> **four are beyond my understanding:**
> [19]**The way an eagle flies in the sky,**
> **the way of a serpent on a rock,**
> **the way of a ship on the high seas,**
> **and the way of a man with a young woman.**
> **Proverbs 30:18-19** (ISV)

The writer is reflecting on four things that inspire wonder for him and one of these is the genuine attraction/love of a man and a woman. It's a wondrous thing, even fascinating. This explains why songs, poems, books and stories throughout human history have focused on the topic (or, at least, include it).

Why are There So Many Interpretations?

Because, as noted in chapter **1**, the Song of Songs is art and art is typically created in such a way to leave room for interpretation.

The nature of song lyrics & poetry is to convey emotions and spur intrigue, images, concepts and lessons above a definitive narrative. It inspires people in different ways and that's what art appreciation is all about.

Joseph Conrad put it like this in response to a reader who inquired about the correct interpretation of one of his stories: "A work of art is very seldom limited to one exclusive meaning and not necessarily tending to a definite conclusion."

4

Key Insights of the Song of Songs

While the Song of Songs is a beautiful love story and work of art, can readers glean insights from it on love, marriage and sex? Absolutely; and we would expect nothing less from the God-breathed Scriptures. After all, what good is the book if we can't get something from it to bless our lives one way or another?

Here are twelve insights to chew on that are timelessly applicable…

Romantic Love & the Corresponding Marriage/Sex are Pure and Beautiful, Not Evil or Embarrassing

There's this false idea that God is anti-sex, but the LORD created both the sex organs and the pleasure of sexual intimacy, not to mention romantic attraction. Romance and eventual consummation is God's gift to be enjoyed within the context of a committed relationship. The devil didn't create any of this, he just perverts it. God is pro-sex, but anti-sexual immorality.

As noted at the end of the last chapter, when the couple finally consummate their marriage (at least according to the maiden's dream) the LORD says "Eat, friends, and drink; drink your fill of love" (5:1), which is basically the Creator's seal of approval. (Again, it's highly unlikely that 'friends' are speaking since they'd be spying on the couple's private lovemaking; by contrast, the LORD is omnipresent and sees all). God was basically saying to them: "Drink up, my children, and enjoy; it is my gift to you."

In short, the Creator desires for spouses to delight in each other.

Sensual Stimulation and Simple Encouragement is Enhanced through Words of Adoration

Learning to focus on your mate's attributes and creatively praising him/her will enrich your relationship and marriage. This is something that should continue as the decades pass and your spouse is no longer in his/her physical prime.

Of course, this doesn't mean that there isn't a time and place for constructive criticism (Proverbs 9:8-9), which is a form of tough love. Spouses should never condone godless carnality in their mates.

True Love Heightens Self-Image and Therefore Confidence

This goes hand-and-hand with the previous. Like the lovers in the song, speak grandly of your mate, as if she's the most amazing woman on Earth (4:1-5) and he can leap over mountains (5:10-16). This will, needless to say, have a positive effect on his/her self-image and will enhance your relationship and intimacy. Anyone who constantly puts down their spouse — whether privately or publicly — will spoil or even destroy the relationship.

Speaking of which, Patti Roberts told the tragic story of her first lovemaking experience with her husband in her book *Ashes to Gold.* As he was lying on the bed and she removed her remaining garments he cluelessly observed, "You know, you look fatter with your clothes off." She was devastated and experienced the sinking feeling that, while they would have sex that night, they would not be lovers. It's incredible the marriage lasted ten years.

In Solomon's song, by contrast, we observe the lovers freely communicating during their make-out session in a mutually encouraging manner (4:1-5:1). They speak unreservedly to each other, which of course doesn't mean you *have* to speak when being affectionate. Yet it shows that we shouldn't allow awkwardness or prudishness to inhibit our verbal communion during intimate moments.

The Love-at-First-Sight Phenomenon

This phenomenon could more accurately be described as wholesale-attraction-at-first-sight, which can ideally develop into deep love and a long-lasting relationship. We observe this with the Shepherd's observation about the Shulammite maiden:

> **You have stolen my heart, my sister, my bride;**
> **you have Stolen my heart**
> **with one glance of your eyes**
> **with one jewel of your necklace**
>
> **Song of Songs 4:9**

This isn't to say that *all* marriages begin with love-at-first-sight. For instance, my mother said she found my dad "egotistical" when she first met him and naturally wasn't attracted to him. My father, however, said he was crazy about mom the second he laid eyes on her. As he pursued her he eventually won her over and they were together till death did them part.

The love-at-first sight phenomenon was obviously one-sided in this case, but it was still key to bringing the two together, without which I wouldn't be writing this. I wouldn't even exist.

Do Not Arouse Love Prematurely

Over and over the Shulammite maiden advises "Do not arouse or awaken love until it so desires" (2:7, 3:5 & 8:4). The Berean Study Bible phrases this as "Do not arouse or awaken love **until the time is right**." In other words, don't be so quick to jump into an intimate romantic relationship. Patiently wait until you're mature enough to discern the worthy soul your heart truly loves and can be committed to for life. Solomon elsewhere wrote "There is a time for everything, and a season for every activity under the heavens" (Ecclesiastes 3:1). The time for a man and woman to enjoy sexual union is marriage, which occurs *after* they've found the worthy one who has genuinely stirred their love.

In short, love must wait for the right soulmate to come along. Don't rush getting married for the sake of getting married. Don't be more enchanted with the *idea* of a wedding and marriage than the person you're marrying. Anyone who does so is setting themselves up for great heartbreak.

This truth is especially apropos in our modern **LIE**beral-influenced culture where teens are pressured by peers and entertainment media to have sex as early as possible and as often as possible (and, even worse, as perverse as possible), which — needless to say — is a recipe for all kinds of unnecessary troubles.

Eros Love is Defined

The Bible reveals that there are four types of love in the human experience (which we'll examine in chapter **8**). Whereas the great love passage, 1 Corinthians 13:4-8, defines *agape* love, which is practical love, the Song of Songs has a verse that expounds on *eros* love, which is romantic love:

> **6 Place me like a seal over your heart,**
> **like a seal on your arm;**
> **for love is as strong as death,**
> **its jealousy unyielding as the grave.**
> **It burns like blazing fire,**
> **like a mighty flame.**
> **7 Many waters cannot quench love;**
> **rivers cannot sweep it away.**
> **If one were to give**
> **all the wealth of one's house for love,**
> **it would be utterly scorned.**
>
> **Song of Songs 8:6-7**

Four qualities of *eros* love are noted:

1. It is as strong and unyielding as death and the grave. In other words, love seals two souls together even as the grave seals the dead.
2. It is like a blazing fire within the person.
3. Figuratively speaking, it's such a mighty inferno that not even rivers of water can quench it.

4. No amount of money can purchase it; it is priceless and can only be given away. Remember the classic song *Can't Buy Me Love?*

Beware of the "Little Foxes" that Can Destroy *Eros* Love and the Relationship

This can be observed in 2:15. Both partners must be on guard against little things that can build-up over time and eventually hinder or even ruin one's relationship with God and his/her spouse. This could be any number of "little" things, such as sloth, lust for others, preference for other things, doubt, a thankless spirit, bitterness, frustration, hatred, porn, materialism or being stubbornly unapologetic.

Keep weeds like this out of your garden, so to speak, and continue to cultivate faith and relationship with God, which naturally has a positive impact on your marriage, especially as the years and decades proceed.[2]

Arranged Marriages are *Not* the Ideal

In Old Testament times arranged marriages were customary in biblical regions and these were organized by the families of the bridegroom and bride in question. Sometimes they were the result of political alliances, such as Solomon's marriage to Pharaoh's daughter (1 Kings 3:1). The obvious problem with such arrangements is that the individual is not *choosing* his/her spouse and so there's a good chance that he/she won't find the other one a

---

[2] For more details see the article (and video) at the Fountain of Life site *Altars & Altar Calls and how they're Relevant*.

fitting or desirable mate-for-life. This is a potential recipe for unhappiness and dissatisfaction, to say the least.

I'm not saying that arranged marriages *can't* work. The best case scenario in an arranged marriage is that the two spouses develop love for each other. But shouldn't the beginning step for a happy marriage be that the man or woman is *attracted to* the spouse and *enjoys* spending time with her/him and vice versa? I'm not talking about mere physical attraction here, but rather all-around physical/mental/spiritual allure.

For instance, I may find Lady Gaga *physically* attractive, but — if I were single — I wouldn't even want to go on a date with her let alone entertain the idea of marrying her. Why? Because I don't find her *inwardly* appealing and we're on different planets *ideologically.*

Another defense for arranged marriages is that fathers & mothers are the ideal people to choose a life-partner for their children. Yet I know (and you know) many fathers and mothers who are the *last* persons on Earth to entrust such an important decision. Personally, I wouldn't want *anyone* else choosing my wife for me, except God. Speaking of which…

Ideally, all Christian marriages should be arranged marriages in the sense that the man and woman have diligently sought their Creator on whom to marry and the Spirit leads them to their future spouse. In essence, **God arranges the marriage**. A good example of this in the Bible is when the LORD orchestrated the marriage of Isaac & Rebekah in Genesis 24.

However, that's not what we're talking about here. We're talking about marriages being contractually arranged by families or regional leaders wherein romantic desire isn't a factor in the negotiation (which, again, isn't to say that such feelings *can't* come later). In these kinds of marriages neither the young woman nor the man pursued each other prior to the arrangement and, often, didn't even know what the other looked like, particularly in cultures where the woman wore a veil.

Yet this is not what we observe in the Song of Songs, which is God's biblical model for romantic love and marriage. The two lovers — who will go on to wed and consummate — are clearly head-over-heels in love with each other. For instance, observe how aggressively the Shulammite woman pursues her shepherd lover in 3:1-4. Even if this sequence is a dream or daydream it reveals her great *longing* for "the one [her] heart loves." Likewise, the man describes the Shulammite in terms of being *intoxicated* by her all-encompassing beauty and love (4:10).

This kind of intense all-around attraction forms the basis for a lasting marriage. We call it the "honeymoon stage." Sure, this stage doesn't last forever, but it's the *foundation* upon which a lasting marriage is set.

For anyone who argues that the relationship of the Shulammite and her shepherd was orchestrated by their families and is therefore an arranged marriage: **1.** The two initially met under an apple tree (8:5b), **2.** they became familiar with each other, **3.** they totally adored one another and **4.** they *wanted* to spend the rest of their lives together as a couple, all of which indicates that their committed relationship wasn't an "arranged marriage" in the sense that we're talking here.

Since the topic of wearing veils was breached above, this is a good place to point out that the Shulammite maiden didn't wear a veil when out amidst the flocks in the Shunem region, which can be observed in 1:7. This explains how the shepherd lover knew her beauty so explicitly. When she asks "Why should I be like a veiled woman beside the flocks of your friends?" it indicates that prostitutes wearing veils wandered from flock to flock looking for shepherds interested in their services (e.g. Genesis 38:15). As a young woman potentially looking for the one man she dearly loved, she didn't want to be mistaken for a loose woman.

Monogamy is the Way to Go, Not Polygamy

The Song of Songs supports the idea that God's best for marriage is monogamy, as clearly detailed in the beginning (Matthew 19:4-6). While the LORD *allowed* Hebrew men to marry multiple wives for a couple reasons, polygamy is *not* God's ideal. Polygamous marriages noted in Scripture suffered contention with the inevitable rivalry of the wives (e.g. 1 Samuel 1:1-8).

Solomon's accumulated wives were his undoing (1 Kings 11:1-4). While Solomon was certainly wise in his early reign (1 Kings 4:29) and he officially advocated monogamy as the ideal (Proverbs 5:18, Ecclesiastes 9:9 & Song of Songs), he foolishly ignored God's scriptural instructions by taking multiple foreign wives (Deuteronomy 17:17 & Exodus 34:15-16).

In the New Covenant the Scriptures instruct that leaders in the Church should have but one spouse (1 Timothy 3:2, 3:12 & Titus 1:6), which was to be an ***example*** to the believers under them (1 Timothy 4:12 & 1 Peter 5:3). So, while the New Testament doesn't outright forbid polygamy, it definitely encourages God's ideal as originally stated in Genesis — one husband, one wife, till death do them part.

But why did the LORD allow polygamy in the Old Testament? A couple reasons come to mind: The world at the time generally consisted of patriarchal societies where females relied on their fathers, brothers and spouses for provision & security. Thus marriage, even if it was polygamous, protected women from a life of destitution, prostitution or enslavement.

Polygamy also expedited God's initial directive to "be fruitful and multiply, and fill the earth" (Genesis 1:28, 9:1 & 9:7) seeing as how husbands could impregnate other wives while one was pregnant. This enabled men to have several kids per year, as opposed to just one, and this facilitated the increase of people on Earth.

Take Care of Your Appearance (Even *After* You've Won Your Bride or Husband)

The shepherd's description of his Shulammite maiden (4:1-5) and her descriptions of him (5:10-16) show that they were careful to look, smell and sound their best for their partner. While this is easy to do during the honeymoon stage of a relationship — which these two were in at the time — it's important to strive to look/smell/sound your best for your partner as the decades progress.

I include "sound" because the maiden describes the mouth of her lover as "sweetness itself" (5:16). Was she describing his literal maw or the sweet, encouraging words that proceeded from it? I believe the latter.

Of course everyone is going to be disheveled & sweaty after doing serious yard work or what have you but, even then, a relatively solid body and a healthy attitude go a long way in keeping one attractive whatever his/her age or body type. The Shulammite says of her lover: "**His arms are rods of gold** set with topaz. **His body is like polished ivory** decorated with lapis lazuli" (5:14).

If you're a man, don't give up on the battle of the bulge. I realize it's tough to keep fit today, especially if you have a sit-down job, but few women want a disagreeable lout as a husband, even if you're in your 50s-70s.

Please don't take this as insensitive to those struggling with weight issues. If a person or couple is okay with being heavy, what's that to me? It's none of my business. I'm just encouraging us to look our best for our spouses, whatever our age and body type. Amen?

Procreation is Not the Main Purpose of Sex

While procreation is certainly important, it's not the main purpose of sex in light of the fact that it's never mentioned as the reason for the couple's physical relationship in the Creator's sole book on romance, marriage and sex in the God-breathed Scriptures (2 Timothy 3:16). In short, the LORD sanctioned and blessed the lovers' romance & sexual intimacy **in and of itself**.

Consider this relevant passage from the biblical book of wisdom:

> **18May your fountain be blessed,**
> **and may you rejoice in the wife of your youth.**
> **19A loving doe, a graceful deer**
> **may her breasts satisfy you always,**
> **may you ever be captivated by her love.**
> **20Why be captivated, my son, by an adulteress?**
> **Why embrace the bosom of another man's wife?**
>
> **Proverbs 5:18-20**

"Fountain" in verse 18 is figurative of a man's wife and the intimacy they share, including sex, which is intended by our Creator to bring pleasure and "satisfy."

Pleasure is only one of three God-given benefits of sex. The other two are intimacy and procreation. Pleasure is noted by Solomon in the above passage while intimacy is inferred. He stresses children in another one of his songs (Psalm 127:3-5).

In contrast to a shallow one-night stand or foolish affair, the marital covenant provides the God-blessed context where physical delight, close fellowship, enjoyment, amusement and security are fully realized.

Your Mate Needs You as a Best Friend, Not Just a Physical Lover

The Shulammite maiden plainly speaks of her lover as her beloved *and* **her friend** (5:16). She certainly wants him for sexual intimacy — and overtly so (7:12-14) (note the reference to mandrakes, an ancient aphrodisiac, as detailed in chapter **10**) — yet she also desires her husband to be a brother to her (8:1-4).

In other words, she wants them to be **playmates**. She feels so comfortable with her committed lover that she can be imaginative & playful, spinning tales, knowing that he will not laugh at her. Wives want their man to open his heart to them, to not just be a caring physical lover — as good as that may be — but a playful sibling and a communicative, imaginative, honest **best friend**. Take heed because truer words have never been spoken.

These twelve points are just a sampling of the great insights about romantic love & marriage contained in the Song of Songs. I'm sure you'll discover more yourself.

5

The Interpretation I Favor and Why

I prefer the three-character version — Interpretation #5 in chapter 2 — because it's the best explanation for the lowly young shepherd in the story, who seems to be a different character from the formidable king of Israel. For instance, this interpretation explains why the ladies of Jerusalem required a description of him, which obviously wouldn't be the case if he were King Solomon. Furthermore, it resolves the issue of God using polygamous Solomon as the key character in a biblical story involving lessons on love and marriage.

Song of Songs 8:5b-7 is key to validating this interpretation. These verses in the culminating chapter convey the conclusion of the love story and point to the purpose for which it was created by Solomon under the moving of the Holy Spirit. The female protagonist is addressing her beloved as the one she had met under the apple tree over a year prior, the one who had initially awakened her love, whereupon she appeals to be placed as a seal on a cord about his neck (a mark of ownership) and as a signet ring on his arm, to be his spouse forever.

In the interim Solomon had met her in the field and was so 'wowed' he naturally wanted to add her to his growing harem and so whisks her off to his royal tents and Jerusalem in order to dazzle her and win her heart. She declines despite the great pressure, including the women of the court who insisted that she now "had it made." Yet she could not forget or forsake her shepherd lover to whom she was pledged, the one her heart loved.

Thus King Solomon, a so-called "lady's man," learns a valuable lesson about true love, i.e. committed love between a man and a woman, which is the way the Creator originally intended it (Genesis 2:24 & Matthew 19:4-6). Solomon's Song of Songs — his "greatest hit" — is thus a lesson to all those who have heard the song, seen the performance, or read the poem (the lyrics) ever since!

For those who argue that it takes too much imagination to read the Song of Songs this way — in other words, they view it as a creative narrative forced into the text — *every* interpretation of this poetic book requires the reader to figure out what character or characters are speaking and to whom.

And more: Are they literally speaking to that person or are their words what's hidden in their heart? In other words, are they imagining the exchange or dreaming it? Remember, the headings you'll find in most versions of the Bible are *not* in the original text and were placed there by translators for readers' convenience.

In short, it's up to us to make educated guesses about *who* is speaking and to *whom*, not to mention *what* is taking place in the setting in question and *where* it's occurring.

A Proposed Synopsis of the Love Triangle Interpretation

I'd like to share just one variation of the three-character interpretation, which is not set-in-stone. It's not my personal take on the story, but rather is roughly based on Finis Dake's reading:

While visiting areas north of Jerusalem and viewing his vineyards, King Solomon is enraptured by an exceptional maiden from Shulem, aka Shunem. The damsel is brought into the king's royal tents where she soliloquizes about her beloved shepherd (1:2-3), beseeching him to come to her rescue (1:4). She counters the disdain of the women of the Jerusalem court (1:6) imploring her shepherd lover to reveal where she might find him (1:7). The ladies respond in irony (1:8) while the king enters conveying his praise to win her heart, but fails (1:9-11).

Dismissed from Solomon's presence at the table, the Shulammite dialogues with her shepherd lover, possibly a reminisced exchange or she's daydreaming (1:12-2:6). She then addresses the young women of the city, charging them not to stir love until the right time and person manifest, citing her beloved shepherd as a praiseworthy example (2:7-14). She also conveys her brothers' hindrances (2:15) and how she waited for her lover to come back in the evening, as well as eventually finding him (2:16-3:5).

Solomon's procession returns from Shunem back to Jerusalem (3:6). His goal is to impress her with his royal glory amidst the splendor of the city & palace (3:1-11). But he is not successful as the shepherd lover has followed the maiden there and arranged a meeting (4:1-5) wherein she reveals that she is anxious to leave the flashy environment and go back to her pastoral locale up north (4:6) to which the shepherd commends her faithfulness (4:7-16).

The maiden dialogues with the ladies of the court, sharing a dream she had about her beloved (5:2-8) as well as describing his attributes to them when pressed (5:9-16). Several of the court women then inquire about the whereabouts of her lover to which she answers (6:1-3).

Still determined to win her heart, Solomon continues one last time with his flatteries and gaudy attractions to persuade her (6:4-7:9). He promises to make her his queen of queens with all the privileges thereof, but she declines his proposal due to her love for another and being promised to him, not to mention the dubiousness of being one wife amongst many if she were to cave to Solomon's offer (7:10-8:4).

Finally convinced, the king dismisses her and she returns to her pastoral abode with her beloved shepherd (8:5-14). They stop at the tree where they initially met and renew their vows to one another (8:5-7). Returning home, her brothers reward her for her honorable conduct, according to their promise (8:8-9).

Again, this reading is simply one interpretation; feel free to tweak it as you feel led. For two proposed outlines of this perspective see the **Appendix**.

Additional Lessons *If* the Love Triangle Theory is Valid

These following insights can be added to the ones chronicled in chapter 4:

- Not all women are materialistic and can be seduced by wealth, social status and charming flatteries.

- Some notable women are faithful to the one their heart loves above the lure of wealth and status.
- Just because a woman is extraordinarily beautiful, it doesn't automatically mean she will allow it to spoil her by making her conceited.
- Some women understand and value the truths of the following potent proverbs:

Better a little with the fear of the Lord
than great wealth with turmoil.
Proverbs 15:16

Better a small serving of vegetables with love
than a fattened calf with hatred.
Proverbs 15:17

Better a dry crust with peace and quiet
than a house full of feasting, with strife.
Proverbs 17:1

My Second Favored Interpretation

If the love triangle view is inaccurate, I'll go with Interpretation #3 wherein the Song of Songs is a fictional work of art featuring an idealized version of King Solomon spiced with bits from his real-life experiences, albeit with the infamous polygamous elements removed.

6

Closing Words on the Song of Songs

Although I favor the three-character interpretation for the reasons stated, I know respectable people, even scholars, who embrace the Solomon's-first-wife view or the Solomon-already-with-a-harem-of-140-women position. Meanwhile the fictional love story account shouldn't be ruled out. By contrast, the "king for a day" perspective doesn't have much credibility.

I supplied the five main interpretations of this epic love song for you to ponder in your studies because it helps to consider all of them before drawing a plausible conclusion. Whatever perspective is true, we can all agree that the Song of Songs is an amazing and unique book of the Bible with several relevant lessons on romance & marriage from which to glean. You don't even have to be cognizant of a rigid interpretation in order to appreciate it and receive from it.

Lastly, **Part I** is not intended to be a substitute for reading the Song of Songs and being blessed by the genius and beauty of the song itself; it's just an educational supplement.

Before closing this part of the book, let's briefly consider the *genre* of the Song of Songs…

7

Forms of ART in the Bible

The Song of Songs belongs to the poetic books of Holy Scripture as it consists of the lyrics to an epic ancient song. This makes it art and thus some observations about art in the Bible are fitting. (If this doesn't interest you, just jump ahead to **Part II**).

The Creator is an Artist

God's imaginative creation of the Universe & Earth and all living things (chronicled in Genesis 1-2) can be described as art; after all, a lot of our art appreciation involves marveling at awesome displays of nature, amazing animals or attractive, charismatic people. This shows that **art *began* with the LORD**, the creator of the heavens & earth and all living creatures (Psalm 146:6), and more: We are to be "*imitators* of God" (Ephesians 5:1).

The First Reference to Art in Relation to Human Beings

The first mention of art as a human work, and even an industry, can be found in the first book of the Bible. (By 'industry' I mean the production of goods or services for people in the community to utilize):

> **Adah gave birth to Jabal; he was the father of those who live in tents and raise livestock. [21] His brother's name was Jubal; he was the father of all who play stringed instruments and pipes. [22]Zillah also had a son, Tubal-Cain, who forged all kinds of tools out of bronze and iron.**
>
> **Genesis 4:20-22**

Three major industries are noted:

1. **Livestock**, which relates to human sustenance.
2. **Music**, which relates to art as a craft and the corresponding human appreciation or entertainment (in the positive sense).
3. **Tool manufacturing**, which relates to technology and human convenience or advancement.

Thus art is cited in the same breath as two other industries vital to human existence.

Furthermore, tool manufacturing and the corresponding technology includes an element of art since various tools and the items created from them are typically made with aesthetics in mind; and are themselves art in a sense. For instance, chairs, tables, desks, shelves, utensils and weapons, like swords. (For anyone who doubts that a chair or table relates to technology, technology is defined as the application of scientific knowledge for practical purposes, so designing and building a wooden chair or table would be an application of technology).

Consider vehicles in the modern era, which are a tool to travel from point A to point B: They *can* be created solely with utilitarian concerns in mind, but that's usually not the case. Manufacturers are also concerned with aesthetics, which explains the existence of car shows.

All three of these industries were birthed at the same time in human history. In other words, people are not meant to just eat and use tools for one purpose or another, they can also create and appreciate art, whether music or otherwise. Speaking of which…

Various Forms of Art Noted in the Bible

Several art forms can be observed in Holy Scripture:

- Music, as noted in the Psalms and the Song of Songs. These songs feature a wide range of expression from praise & worship and historical commentary to emotional venting and *(gasp!)* romantic expression.
- Poetry, such as the book of Job, Ecclesiastes and the poetry used throughout the prophetic books.
- Fictional stories, like Christ's parables and Jotham's fantastical tale (Judges 9:8-15).
- Visual arts, including graphical, sculptural, crafts, décor and architectural (1 Kings 6). This would include the aesthetic appeal of the Ark of the Covenant and the Tent Tabernacle (Exodus 25-26).
- The aesthetic element in tools, weapons, armor and so on would fall within the parameters of visual art.

- Performance art, as observed with Isaiah walking around partially nude and barefoot for three years (Isaiah 20), Jeremiah creating and wearing a yoke, which was destroyed by another prophet to symbolize the breaking of the yoke of the king of Babylon (Jeremiah 27-28) and Ezekiel "sieging Jerusalem" and lying on his side for long periods of time, etc. (Ezekiel 4-5). Obviously art can be used as a tool to minister truth to others.
- As noted in chapter **1**, since the Song of Songs contains multiple speaking parts, including choruses of people, it's likely that it was acted out as a musical, likely during the week-long wedding celebration. Keep in mind that poetry, songs and stories were entertainment in ancient times, just as concerts, films and TV programs are to us today.
- Dance would be a form of performance art. Ecclesiastes 3:4 says there is "a time to weep and a time to laugh, a time to mourn and **a time to dance**." Meanwhile the Psalms encourage us to praise the LORD with dancing and music (Psalm 149:3 & 150:4). David danced before the LORD with all his heart, which some naturally took in the wrong spirit (2 Samuel 6:14-23). Aren't there always those types who take offense to an artist despite perfectly noble intentions?

All of these art forms separate human beings from animals. Beasts do not create or perform with aesthetics in mind, even if what they create for practical purposes can be deemed artistic by people, such as a spider's web. Again, art is as intrinsic to the human experience as food and technology.

Lifeless Legalists Tend to Sneer at Art and Those Involved in the Arts

To be expected, people with a Pharisaical spirit tend to look down on some forms or genres of art because it brings pleasure and heightens the appreciation of life whereas religious legalists are by nature life-stifling and growth-stultifying. But, as you can see from the Scriptures, art is inherent to God's nature and, as such, many forms of it can be seen throughout the Bible. Moreover, we are created in God's image and expected to imitate our Creator.

Speaking of which…

God's "Art" Declares the Glory of the Creator

It was pointed out earlier that God's physical creation — the Universe, Earth and all living things — is *the LORD's* art and it is on display to humanity every day, testifying to the Creator's existence and glory despite the creation's fallen state (Romans 1:20 & Psalm 19:1-4).

Have you ever heard a great song or seen it performed live and felt an awe of the artist who composed/performed it? The same principle is at play when you gaze into the starry panorama or feast your eyes on a magnificent vista or marvel at a stunning person or a fascinating animal. All of these things declare the glory of the Creator and inspire awe.

The art you or I create can also inspire awe and "speak" of innumerable worthy things or issues, but the most important one is declaring God's glory or simply truth (reality) in one way or another, covertly or overtly. By doing this we are imitating God as we are called to do.

But, in order for art to be effective…

Artists must "Understand the Times"

The Bible points out that the men of Issachar "understood the times and knew what Israel should do" (1 Chronicles 12:32), which shows that they comprehended the historical context of the current culture and what to do or not do from a godly perspective. Just so, Christian artists in the modern era have to grasp what's happening in their culture or subculture in order to effectively engage people with their art, whatever form that might be.

For instance, it's unlikely that Christians are going to effectively reach lost or searching youths ingrained in Goth rock, hip-hop or extreme metal subcultures with traditional gospel music, like The Gaithers. Not that there's anything wrong with traditional gospel (or The Gaithers), but you have to know your audience and what's trending to successfully reach people and communicate with your art. What's "hip" in one decade is usually not "hip" in the next.

Creating Art *is* Work

Artists are typically looked-down upon by more utilitarian types. They don't view the creation or performance of art to be "real work" nor do they think that the art industry — any form — is essential to life on Earth. But, as noted above, the very beginning of the book of Genesis shows that art was one of the three main industries in the beginning stages of humanity (Genesis 4:20-22).

Furthermore, God's conception of the Universe & Earth and all living things is the most imaginative, awe-inspiring piece of art ever created. Notice what the Bible says about this masterwork:

> **Thus the heavens and the earth were completed in all their vast array.**
> **2By the seventh day God had finished the work he had been doing; so on the seventh day he rested from all his work. 3Then God blessed the seventh day and made it holy, because on it he rested from all the work of creating that he had done.**
>
> **Genesis 2:1-3**

The Scriptures refer to the LORD's creation of the greatest piece of art as "work," which took six days to complete. We marvel at innumerable parts of this "piece" every day one way or another. For instance, we regularly gaze in awe at photographs, paintings, books or movies showcasing breathtaking vistas, amazing animals or striking people — or we appreciate them firsthand — either way, we're blessed by God's art on a daily basis.

The point is that creating great art *is* work. It was work even *before* creation was cursed due to sin (Genesis 3:14-20). Now it's even *more* work because of the Genesis Curse. And Adam's descendants have worked within the context of this negative legacy ever since, which includes you and me. But there's good news…

Christ worked as a carpenter up until the age of 30; his former neighbors in Nazareth recognized him by his prior occupation (Mark 6:3 & Matthew 13:55). The Greek word for 'carpenter' is *tektón (TEK-tohn)*, which refers to a craftsman, carpenter or artisan. *Tektón* is where we get the words tectonic and architect. In 1st Century Israel a *tektón* was a general craftsman who worked with wood, stone or metal in building projects, small or large. In other words, Christ did more than make tables & chairs.

Quality carpenters/builders/architects today make good money, as do people of any profession that takes skill and is in demand, including proficient artists (Proverbs 22:29). As noted earlier, there's a creative element to carpentry and architecture. Imagine how skilled the Messiah was as a builder since he created the Universe, Earth & all living things (Colossians 1:16-17)!

Jesus then worked as a fulltime minister for three and a half years before he was crucified and he was the greatest minister that's ever walked the Earth. Anyone who says effective ministry isn't work doesn't know what they're talking about. It explains why Christ took the apostles on a retreat to the town of Bethsaida after they returned from days of ministering from town to town (Luke 9:10).

Moreover, there's a creative element to ministry, including the imagination necessary to come up with original teachings and parables, not to mention ministering via performance art as Jeremiah and Ezekiel did. In short, ministry includes an artistic aspect.

Whatever work you do, including artistic work, Colossians 3:23 instructs us to:

1. **Work as if working for the Lord**, which is also reflected in Ephesians 6:7.
2. **Do it with all your heart**, which is also reflected in Ecclesiastes 9:10. The lesson? Give it your all; don't just go through the motions or wing it.

In addition, Proverbs 12:24 says that "diligent hands will rule" and Proverbs 22:29 illustrates that those who perfect their craft will be successful within that context; in other words, your work will be in demand however large or small your niche audience may be.

Apply these principles in your work & artistic endeavors and you'll be blessed despite the Genesis Curse while looking forward to the New Heavens and New Earth, the eternal home of righteousness where there will be "**no more curse**" (2 Peter 3:13 & Revelation 22:3).

PART II

Issues Related to Love, Marriage and Sex

Solomon's Song of Songs is just a springboard into the topics of love, marriage and sex. So let's now delve deeper into these matters, including addressing some issues most ministers don't like to talk about because they're too private, awkward or what have you.

It goes without saying that some of these miscellaneous topics (and their corresponding chapters) you'll find of interest while others you won't. Certain subjects you might have an aversion to and understandably so. Pick and choose accordingly.

8

The Four Types of Love

While this book is mainly about romantic love, aka *eros* love, it helps to understand all four types of love featured in the Bible. So let's look at the four Greek words for love and how these four kinds of love are chronicled in the Scriptures:

1. *Storge* Love

***Storge* love** is familial love, which refers to the bond, affection and loyalty that develops between family members. Although the word itself, *storge (STOR-gay),* is not found in the Bible we see numerous examples of it, like Martha & Mary's love for their brother Lazarus in John 11.

Unfortunately the opposite can happen, which is when family members develop *hatred* for each other. Some good examples of this include: Cain & Abel (Genesis 4:1-11) and Joseph & his jealous brothers (Genesis 37).

2. *Phileo* Love

***Phileo* love** is friendship love or brotherly love like the platonic affection of David and Jonathan (2 Samuel 1:25-26). Philadelphia, "the city of brotherly love," was named after this type of love. You could say that *phileo* love is *storge* love applied to non-family members or that *storge* love is *phileo* love applied to family members. In either case, there's an element of "tender affection" or a bond, respect.

The word *phileo (fil-LAY-oh)* can be found some 25 times in the original Greek text of the New Testament whereas the noun form, *philia (fil-EE-ah),* appears much less often (which explains why we're calling it *phileo* love).

Jesus' love for Martha, Mary and Lazarus is a good example of *phileo* love, as observed here:

> [5] **Now Jesus loved** *(agape)* **Martha and her sister and Lazarus…**
> [35] **Jesus wept.** [36] **Then the Jews said, "See how he loved** *(phileo)* **him!"**
>
> **John 11:5, 35-36**

Verse 5 establishes that Christ loved the three siblings with *agape* love, which refers to practical love (this will be explained momentarily). Yet verse 36 reveals more specifically that the Lord loved Lazarus with *phileo* love, meaning he had tender affection & respect for him, as if Lazarus was his brother.

3. *Eros* Love

***Eros* love** is *phileo* love between members of the opposite sex and includes a romantic element, but it doesn't refer to shallow sexual lust. Although the word *eros (eer-ROSS)* doesn't appear in the original manuscripts there are many examples of this type of love in Scripture. One overt example can be observed in the amazing Song of Songs. Here's a passionate expression of love in that book where the man is speaking to the woman:

> **show me your face,**
> **let me hear your voice;**
> **for your voice is sweet,**
> **and your face is lovely.**
>
> **Song of Songs 2:14**

4. *Agape* Love

***Agape* love** is simply practical love or love-in-action and is therefore not dependent on affection or respect. This can be observed in the Scriptural definition of *agape* love found in 1 Corinthians 13:4-7, which says that *agape* love is patient, kind, does not envy, does not boast, is not proud, is not rude or selfish or easily angered, etc.

The word 'love' for God's love for the world in the most popular passage of the Bible is *agape (uh-GAHP-ay):*

> **For God so <u>loved</u> the world that he gave his one and only Son, that whoever believes in him shall not perish but have eternal life.**
>
> **John 3:16**

The Creator was walking in love toward all humanity when the Father allowed the Son to die in our place as our substitutionary death. This was *agape* love, practical love, and not *phileo* love.

Phileo Love is Not Necessary to *Agape* Love Someone

With this understanding, you don't have to have *phileo* love for people — affection or respect — in order to *agape* love them. Why? Because *agape* love refers to practical love and has little to do with affection, that is, liking the person.

This explains how we can fulfill Jesus & Paul's instructions to love our enemies (Luke 6:27 & Romans 12:20-21). Do you like your enemies, that is, *phileo* love them? Of course not. But this isn't a problem because **we are not commanded to *phileo* love our enemies, we're told to *agape* love them**. Are you following? This explains why *agape* love is often defined as "unconditional love" since it is practical in nature and, again, not dependent upon liking an individual or on how well they treat you.

However, I should stress that *agape* love does not refer to only the nicey-wicey form of love. *Agape* love is love-in-action and refers to doing the kind thing, the good thing for the person in question. Are you truly being kind or good by condoning something that will eventually ruin or destroy a person? Or, worse, enabling them? Obviously not.

This explains how Jesus — who is love because "God is love" (1 John 4:8) — was able to chase the fools out of the Temple with a whip, yelling and throwing over tables (Mark 11:15-18). Or when he rebuked Peter as "satan" (Matthew 16:23). His actions may not have been nice, but they were kind and good because they benefited the people.[3]

In light of all this, allow me to point something out that you won't hear very often: The LORD ***is*** *agape* love and so God loves *(agape)* the world, just as the most popular passages states, John 3:16. What this means is that God is extending practical love to all human beings even though unbelievers are un-regenerated "objects of wrath" (Ephesians 2:1-5). For instance, I was only saved and "made alive with Christ" because of God's great *agape* love!

But God doesn't *phileo* love everyone, that is, have tender affection or respect for them. He doesn't have a close bond with everyone. For instance, do you think God is up there observing the many pedophile priests and saying, "Oh, I just have so much warm affection for these sick perverts?" Do you think the LORD was close buddies with Hitler? Of course not.

Come Near to God and He will Come Near to YOU

The Bible says that the Father *phileo* loved Jesus when Christ was on Earth (John 5:19-20). Why? Because Jesus imitated the Father, that is, he was godly — *like God.* As such, the Messiah grew in God's favor (Luke 2:52). We too can grow in God's favor by coming near to the LORD (James 4:8, 2 Peter 3:18 & Eph. 5:1).

Think about it in terms of a "teacher's pet," in a positive way. The pupil is the teacher's pet because she honors the teacher and is compliant. She does her homework and strives to do well on tests. If she offends the teacher she readily apologizes. The teacher will

---

[3] See the article *Gentle Love and Tough Love* at the FOL site for more details.

naturally have *phileo* love for such a student — affection and respect — but not for a student who's aloof and shows contempt.

Of course the teacher will care about the latter student because the noble teacher unbiasedly cares about all his students. He wants each one to learn, develop and be successful in life. But when the student is foolish and disrespectful there's only so much the teacher can do.

The teacher will walk in *agape* love toward such students — practical love — but the teacher will not have *phileo* love for them. Why? Because they're fools who regard the teacher with contempt. All the teacher can do is continue walking in *agape* love toward them — including praying for them, and even implementing tough love when appropriate — in the hope that they'll positively respond at some point and turn from their folly.

As amazing as it sounds, YOU can grow in God's *phileo* love! "Come near to God and he will draw near to YOU." It's an *axiom* — a universal law. Strive for a closer relationship with your Creator. Cultivate a more intimate prayer life, which is simply talking with God. Paul instructed us to "pray without ceasing," which indicates a 24/7 bond of communion (1 Thessalonians 5:17).

Love God by obeying his instruction, both the general instructions from the *written* Word and the specific instructions of the *living* Word, the Spirit of Christ (1 John 5:3). As you do this you'll **grow in God's favor** just as surely as Jesus Christ did when he was on Earth (Luke 2:52) and others as well, like Samuel (1 Samuel 2:26).

Peter put it like this:

> **But grow in the grace** [favor] **and knowledge of our Lord and Savior Jesus Christ. To him be glory both now and forever! Amen.**
>
> **2 Peter 3:18**

Just as important as it is to grow in the *knowledge* of the Lord, it's also vital to grow in God's *grace;* that is, God's **favor**.

9

Beauty, Objectification and Lust

The Bible plainly acknowledges the beauty or handsomeness of certain people on several occasions. For instance, the following verses reveal that Sarai (aka Sarah), Rebekah, Rachel and Esther were women of exceptional beauty:

> **When Abram came to Egypt, the Egyptians saw that Sarai was a very beautiful woman.**
>
> **Genesis 12:14**

> **Before he had finished praying, Rebekah came out with her jar on her shoulder. She was the daughter of Bethuel son of Milkah, who was the wife of Abraham's brother Nahor. [16] The woman was very beautiful, a virgin; no man had ever slept with her. She went down to the spring, filled her jar and came up again.**
>
> **Genesis 24:15-16**

> **When the men of that place asked him about his wife, he said, "She is my sister," because he was afraid to say, "She is my wife." He thought, "The men of this place might kill me on account of Rebekah, because she is beautiful."**
>
> **Genesis 26:7**

> **Leah had weak eyes, but Rachel had a lovely figure and was beautiful.**
>
> **Genesis 29:17**

> **Mordecai had a cousin named Hadassah, whom he had brought up because she had neither father nor mother. This young woman, who was also known as Esther, had a lovely figure and was beautiful. Mordecai had taken her as his own daughter when her father and mother died.**
>
> **Esther 2:7**

And here are a few passages that reveal how Joseph, Saul and David were exceptionally good-looking men:

> **So Potiphar left everything he had in Joseph's care; with Joseph in charge, he did not concern himself with anything except the food he ate.**
> **Now Joseph was well-built and handsome, [7]and after a while his master's wife took notice of Joseph and said, "Come to bed with me!"**
>
> **Genesis 39:6-7**

> **Kish had a son named Saul, as handsome a young man as could be found anywhere in Israel, and he was a head taller than anyone else.**
>
> **1 Samuel 9:2**

So he sent for him [David] **and had him brought in. He was glowing with health and had a fine appearance and handsome features. Then the LORD said, "Rise and anoint him; this is the one."**

1 Samuel 16:12

Appreciating Beauty vs. Objectifying a Person

To objectify a person means to degrade an individual to the status of a mere object. The Bible offers an interesting lesson on objectification in this account of King Xerxes of Persia and his queen, Vashti:

On the seventh day, when King Xerxes was in high spirits from wine, he commanded the seven eunuchs who served him—Mehuman, Biztha, Harbona, Bigtha, Abagtha, Zethar and Karkas—[11]to bring before him Queen Vashti, wearing her royal crown, in order to display her beauty to the people and nobles, for she was lovely to look at. [12]But when the attendants delivered the king's command, Queen Vashti refused to come. Then the king became furious and burned with anger.

Esther 1:10-12

Basically Xerxes wanted to "show off" his wife to all the partying elites at his banquet because she was extraordinarily beautiful, but Vashti was so repulsed by the idea of being objectified by her husband's drunken guests she was willing to risk her queen-ship and be deposed, which is what happened. (This of course paved the way for Esther, a secret Hebrew, to become queen of Persia, as observed in Esther 2:17).

To disobey a direct order from the king in that culture was unthinkable, but Vashti obviously couldn't betray her own dignity — i.e. violate her conscience — to be ogled by a bunch of drunken men, especially considering the possibility that she was to appear before them *wearing only her crown*, which is what some Hebrew historians maintain. This account is contrasted by Salome's willingness to dance at King Herod's banquet but, then, she didn't do it nude and she & her mother had an ulterior motive (Mark 6:17-28).

What can we get from Vashti's impressive refusal to give-in to her husband's ignoble request at great cost? While it's nice to be sincerely noticed or complimented now and then, being objectified is a different story. It reduces the person to a piece of meat and the Bible emphasizes that this is a worldly perspective rather than spiritual (2 Corinthians 5:16).

'What about "Beauty is in the Eye of the Beholder"?'

Obviously there is such a thing as exceptional good-looks, but beauty is also subjective. For instance, an Aborigine living in the bush might likely find a beauty contest winner in the USA or Europe unappealing and understandably so. What makes his idea of beauty less valid than a judge at a beauty contest in Western Civilization? Every person is like that Aborigine: **The only beauty that matters to the individual is what *he* or *she* finds beautiful**, not what some judge at a beauty contest or magazine editor insists is beautiful. Hence, beauty is in the eye of the beholder.

So beauty is both subjective and objective. It is subjective in that people are unique individuals who don't find the same things attractive; they each have their own opinions and preferences on what is beautiful or handsome. However, beauty is also objective in that some people are simply better looking than the average person, as noted in the scriptures cited above.

Are there examples of subjective beauty in the Bible? Yes. The male protagonist in the Song of Songs refers to his beloved like so:

Like a lily among thorns
is my darling among the young women.
Song of Songs 2:2

You are altogether beautiful, my darling;
<u>there is no flaw in you</u>.
Song of Songs 4:7

He speaks of his beloved's beauty as if she blows away all other women on Earth, even to the point of having "*no flaw.*" Meanwhile King Solomon calls her his "*perfect* one" (Song of Songs 6:9). Is this factually true or merely the subjective perspective of these men looking through the lens of passionate romantic love (or, in Solomon's case, lustful infatuation)? Obviously the latter since even the most beautiful women in this fallen world have flaws.[4]

The woman in the story speaks of her man in a similar idealized fashion, e.g. Song of Songs 5:10-16.

---

[4] In this particular paragraph I'm speaking as if the love triangle interpretation is true, obviously because it's the perspective I favor. If this interpretation is inaccurate, however, then Solomon is presumably the sole male speaking in these verses.

While both ‘lover’ and ‘beloved’ in the Song of Songs may have been exceptional in one way or another, neither were the most attractive, flawless male or female on Earth. As such, these verses reflect the idea of subjective beauty.

‘What about <u>Inner</u> Beauty?’

What good is outer beauty without *inner* beauty to balance it out? If anything, inner beauty is more important and very much so. After all, what benefit would it be to marry a gorgeous Hollywood starlet or stud who has a roaming eye and the marriage lasts a short time due to inevitable unfaithfulness?

This explains why Peter, inspired by the Holy Spirit, encouraged female believers to *not* focus on “outward adornment” and all that goes with it, but rather on the true attractiveness of “your inner self, the unfading beauty of a gentle and quiet spirit, which is of great worth in God’s sight” (1 Peter 1:3-4). He wasn’t saying female believers can’t wear attractive clothing, just that their focus should be on the true beauty that stems from a spiritual heart.

This is what attracted me to Carol when I first met her. Of course I found her physically attractive, but she didn’t dress like a courtesan and didn’t need to. It was her gentle, quiet, godly spirit that shined like the midday sun and captured my attention. The back cover photo is us on our wedding day in July, 1995.

By “gentle” and “quiet” I don’t mean Carol was a shy pushover, I mean she wasn’t an obnoxious loudmouth, like odious **LIE**berals and their opinionated falsities & slander. There’s a pleasantness to a gentle, quiet spirit that doesn’t constantly bloviate and isn’t rash with jumping to conclusions. At the same time Carol has no qualms about wisely holding me accountable to the Word of God;

and I do the same with her, which is a form of tough love. This kind of love doesn't fail to correct others when necessary (Proverbs 27:5,17).

But the Scriptures don't just encourage *women* to be gentle and quiet as these are positive attributes for *both* men and women. For instance, Paul said to *all* the believers at Philippi: "Let your gentleness be evident to all" (Philippians 4:5). Meanwhile James said "**Everyone** should be quick to listen, slow to speak and slow to become angry" (James 1:19). And the book of Proverbs says "The one who has knowledge <u>uses words with restraint</u>, and whoever has understanding is <u>even-tempered</u>" (Proverbs 17:27).

In other words, the Scriptures exhort *both* men and women to **not** be loathsome loudmouths. Yet this doesn't mean there isn't a time & place for righteous reprimand and Holy Ghost-inspired preaching.

Appreciating Beauty vs. Lusting

Since the Bible clearly acknowledges physical beauty or handsomeness in human beings, and God created this beauty, there's a place for appreciating it, whether being awed by it or simply admiring it. There's nothing wrong with this. As the Scripture says, "**To the pure, all things are pure**" (Titus 1:15).

However, the Bible condemns lust for anyone outside the covenant of holy matrimony, which is preoccupation in thought or deed with sexual desire and has to do with the aforementioned objectification. Even for your wife or husband, your desire for her/him should be greater than one-dimensional lust or the marriage won't likely last. Christ said, "I tell you that anyone who looks at a woman lustfully has already committed adultery with her in his heart" (Matthew 5:28). This explains why righteous Job made an agreement with his eyes to not look at a woman lustfully (Job 31:1).

But what is the dividing line between appreciating beauty and sexual lust? Here's a parable to illustrate the difference:

You're walking down the sidewalk and come across a bed of flowers in which you naturally relish their colorful beauty and fragrance. You may stop for a moment, but you continue on your way because you have a schedule and other things to do, not to mention the flowers aren't yours. Then someone else walks down the sidewalk and sees the same beautiful bed of flowers, but he dives into it and wildly pulls out the flowers by the roots so he can take them home with him. I think it's obvious which one of these is reasonable, acceptable behavior and which is not.

If that's not clear enough, here's a more blunt way to distinguish falling into lust: If your thoughts about a person inspire you to run to a secluded room to gratify yourself, it's obviously lust. The answer to this kind of problem is learning to control your thoughts, as well as learning to walk in the spirit (which is covered in detail in chapter **15**). God said to Cain: "sin is crouching at your door; it desires to have you, **but you must master it**" (Genesis 4:7).

All men and women are unique with different strengths or weaknesses and each one is going to have to determine in their relationship with God what the dividing line is between appreciating beauty and lust. It's a personal matter between the individual and the LORD, not to mention a part of "working out your salvation with fear and trembling" (Philippians 2:12).

Let me close with this relevant story filled with insights:

Several years ago I was part of a men's group that would read Christian books on male-oriented issues and discuss them. In one of the books the author went to extreme lengths to protect himself from his lust problem. For instance, before reading a newspaper or magazine he'd cut out any ads or pictures that featured a fetching female, especially scantily-clad ones, like underwear or bathing suit ads. In addition, if he were out in public he'd never look at a comely female for more than a passing glance (approximately 0.187 seconds) and would refuse to view TV shows or movies that showed women in alluring apparel. Etcetera.

These were rules that this man came up with in order to walk free of lust and serve the Lord with a clear conscience. There's nothing wrong with this if a man has issues with lust, usually due to an exceptional sex drive. Such a man observes these kind of rules for the sake of personal holiness, which is pure religion in God's eyes (James 1:27). Such rules are akin to the alcoholic who must stay away from any environment that includes alcoholic beverages in order to walk in victory. But not all men have such a weakness to lust, nor do all people struggle with alcohol like the severe alcoholic.

To be expected, this topic provoked a lively discussion at the group. A couple of the men, both married, admitted that they needed to go to such extremes to walk free of lust, while some others felt the rules were so radical that it was the next thing to requiring women to wear robes and veils in public, like in some Islamic countries.

This was the perfect occasion for us to practice Paul's instructions in Romans 14: The men who felt it necessary to adhere to these rigid rules should not look down on those who didn't and vice versa. As Paul instructed, "Who are you to judge someone else's servant? To his own master he stands or falls. And he will stand, for the Lord is able to make him stand… Each one should be fully convinced in his own mind" (Romans 14:4-5).

Such rules are fine if you require them to keep a clean conscience before God, but be careful that religious pride doesn't seep-in and you start judging and condemning other genuine believers who don't require these rules. Otherwise you'll be infected by legalism, which is a path of spiritual darkness and death even though it wraps itself in the garnishment of respectable religiosity.

Carol & I attended one assembly where the pastor had a history of alcohol-related problems before he came to the Lord and, consequently, was hell-bent against anything having to do with alcohol. Not only was drinking a sip of alcohol a sin — to *him* — it was also a sin to dine at an establishment that served alcohol, like Red Lobster. In fact, it was wrong to shop at a store that sold alcohol, like Walmart! Do you see the problem here? Because he had a weakness toward alcohol he developed an extreme view on the subject and tried to impose *his* personal rules of holiness on everyone else, including the vast majority who had no need of such radical rules.

Just so there's no misunderstanding about alcohol in this book, let's briefly go off-topic and look at…

Drinking an Alcoholic Beverage vs. Being a Drunkard

Drinking an alcoholic beverage is not a sin in and of itself. But it can be a sin — or, at least, unwise — for certain people or in certain environments, not to mention anything done without moderation becomes negative by default.

Obviously someone with an alcoholic past must stay away from alcoholic beverages altogether, just as a man with a severe lust problem has to stay away from pictures or shows/movies that feature scantily clad females. It's just common sense: If your flesh has a weakness for something, you wisely avoid anything that would stir it up and lead to a fall.

Yet Christ didn't completely abstain from alcohol (Matthew 11:19) and Paul instructed Timothy to drink a little wine apparently for health reasons (1 Timothy 5:23). Moreover, the LORD permitted the Hebrews to drink fermented beverages at certain celebrations (Deuteronomy 14:26). This somewhat corresponds to the Messiah's first miracle — turning water into wine at a wedding celebration, which obviously wasn't grape juice (John 2:1-11).

Yet "Scripture interprets Scripture" and so these passages need balanced out by others, like Proverbs 20:1, 23:20, 23:30-32 and this verse:

> **Do not get drunk on wine, which leads to debauchery.**
>
> **Ephesians 5:18**

So the issue isn't the alcoholic beverage itself, but rather the individual who loses a proper sense of moderation (self-control) and, instead, becomes controlled by the alcohol, meaning drunk. Why is this wrong or unwise? Because drunkenness naturally "leads to debauchery," which means decadence, aka immorality; in short, sin.

Yet there's nothing wrong with drinking an alcoholic beverage and stopping, as long as you don't make a weak brother or sister fall by your actions, which is what Paul was talking about in Romans 14:13-23. Why risk making a believer with a weak conscience or a weakness for alcohol stumble due to your actions? It's a matter of selfless **love for others**, which trumps personal freedom and corresponds to the New Covenant law of Christ or law of love (Galatians 6:2 & 1 Corinthians 9:21), which we'll look at in chapter **15**.[5]

[5] For more on the topic of alcohol see the article *Can Christians Drink Alcoholic Beverages?* at the FOL site.

10

What are "Mandrakes" Mentioned in the Bible?

"Mandrakes" are cited in the Bible five times including once in the Song of Songs (7:13).[6] They refer to the roots of mandrake plants, which sometimes resemble naked humans, particularly the lower areas. They were used as an aphrodisiac and to induce pregnancy, as observed in this passage:

> **When Rachel saw that she was not bearing Jacob any children, she became jealous of her sister. So she said to Jacob, "Give me children, or I'll die!"**
> **2Jacob became angry with her and said, "Am I in the place of God, who has kept you from having children?"...**
> **14During wheat harvest, Reuben went out into the fields and found some mandrake plants, which he brought to his mother Leah. Rachel**

---

[6] The Hebrew word for mandrakes, *duday (doo-DAH-ee)*, is also used in Jeremiah 24:1, but in that context it refers to baskets.

> **said to Leah, "Please give me some of your son's mandrakes."**
> **[15]But she said to her, "Wasn't it enough that you took away my husband? Will you take my son's mandrakes too?"**
> **"Very well," Rachel said, "he can sleep with you tonight in return for your son's mandrakes."**
> **[16]So when Jacob came in from the fields that evening, Leah went out to meet him. "You must sleep with me," she said. "I have hired you with my son's mandrakes." So he slept with her that night…**
> **[22]Then God remembered Rachel; he listened to**
> **her and enabled her to conceive. [23]She became**
> **pregnant and gave birth to a son and said, "God**
> **has taken away my disgrace." [24]She named him**
> **Joseph, and said, "May the Lord add to me another son."**
>
> **Genesis 30:1-2,14-16,22-24**

Jacob, if you don't remember, was renamed Israel by the LORD shortly later (Genesis 32:22-32). He favored his wife Rachel, but she wasn't able to bear children for him and so she made a bargain with her older sister, Leah — also married to Jacob — to allow Leah to sleep with Jacob in exchange for the mandrake plants that Leah's son had found.

The passage doesn't say that the Mandrake roots actually worked to induce pregnancy, just that "God remembered Rachel" and thus enabled her to conceive her son Joseph. Nevertheless, it's clear that mandrake roots were thought to augment sex & procreation and were sought after for this purpose.

As noted, Mandrake roots sometimes look like nude bodies, particularly the nether regions. So the fact that they were used as an aphrodisiac and to induce pregnancy would be a natural correlation.

Think about it in terms of walnuts, which resemble human brains when cracked open; they're coincidentally the top nut for brain health. Similarly, tomatoes resemble the heart when opened up — the "chambers," etc. — and they're by happenstance strategic to cardiac health. Is this mere coincidence or did God do this purposely?

The fact that **1.** the LORD created mandrake roots, **2.** they're cited in Holy Scripture five times, **3.** they resemble the lower regions of naked humans and **4.** were used to augment sex & procreation shows that the Almighty is an imaginative Creator, not to mention has a sense of humor.

Do mandrake roots actually "work"? I have no idea, but Rachel obviously *believed* they did; and belief is faith, which opens the door to the miraculous (e.g. Mark 5:34 & 10:52).[7]

[7] For important insights on faith & healing see the article *Healing — How Do I Receive?* at the FOL site (as well as the corresponding video).

11

What IS Marriage? (and Related Topics)

Marriage was defined by our Creator at the very beginning of physical creation:

> **That is why a man leaves his father and mother and is united to his wife, and they become one flesh.**
>
> **Genesis 2:24**

Christ confirmed this definition:

> **"Haven't you read," he replied, "that at the beginning the Creator 'made them male and female,' [5]and said, 'For this reason a man will leave his father and mother and be united to his wife, and the two will become one flesh'? [6]So they are no longer two, but one flesh. Therefore what God has joined together, let no one separate."**
>
> **Matthew 19:4-6**

This definition is also conveyed in Mark 10:6-9 while Paul confirmed it in Ephesians 5:31.

What we conclude from this is that **marriage is a lifelong-committed relationship between a biological man and a biological woman, which makes them "one flesh" in God's eyes**. It's a *covenant* between a man and a woman — a vital and enduring social contract (Proverbs 2:17). We observe this in the divinely-orchestrated marriage of Isaac and Rebecca:

> **Isaac brought her into the tent of his mother Sarah, and he married Rebekah. So she became his wife, and he loved her; and Isaac was comforted after his mother's death.**
>
> **Genesis 24:67**

Notice that there was no wedding ceremony in the conventional sense that we understand today; the marriage was official due to the agreement between the two families and, most importantly, Isaac and Rebecca. The financial arrangements were established beforehand. There was no minister or judge required to pronounce them husband & wife and no written document is mentioned. The couple and their families had a verbal contract, a financial agreement and Isaac & Rebecca's decisive willingness (Amos 3:3).

The bottom line is that this is what a marriage is: **A man and a woman *agreeing* to be united as man & wife — "one flesh" — as long as they live.** It's a lifelong commitment between a biological male and female (which automatically discounts the idea of same-sex marriage, i.e. "gay" marriage).

While being "one flesh" presumes sexual intercourse will occur, that is not the definition of marriage, as Joseph was married to Mary *before* consummation, as observed here:

This is how the birth of Jesus the Messiah came
about: His mother Mary was pledged to be
married to Joseph, but before they came
together, she was found to be pregnant through
the Holy Spirit. 19 Because Joseph her husband
was faithful to the law, and yet did not want to
expose her to public disgrace, he had in mind to
divorce her quietly.
20 But after he had considered this, an angel of
the Lord appeared to him in a dream and said,
"Joseph son of David, do not be afraid to take
Mary home as your wife, because what is
conceived in her is from the Holy Spirit. 21 She
will give birth to a son, and you are to give him
the name Jesus, because he will save his people
from their sins."
22 All this took place to fulfill what the Lord had
said through the prophet: 23 "The virgin will
conceive and give birth to a son, and they will
call him Immanuel" (which means "God with
us").
24 When Joseph woke up, he did what the angel
of the Lord had commanded him and took Mary
home as his wife. 25 But he did not consummate
their marriage until she gave birth to a son. And
he gave him the name Jesus.

Matthew 1:18-25

This makes sense because, if sexual intercourse was the sole definition of marriage — of being "one flesh" — then couples would no longer be married if they ceased having intercourse, such as older couples or cases wherein either husband or wife cannot have sex for one reason or another.

This biblical definition of marriage shows that a man and woman could legitimately marry in a remote location, such as if they were castaways on a deserted island or settlers in remote areas of the globe. But, obviously, they'd want to make it legal if/when they returned to civilization. Speaking of which…

Why Make Marriage "Legal"?

Answer: Because **1.** believers are to be submitted to the righteous laws of the governing authorities (Romans 13:1-6) and **2.** to avoid "all appearance of evil" (1 Thessalonians 5:22 KJV). The latter is important in order to be an effective witness to others (2 Corinthians 8:21).

The former is important because it reveals the couple's willingness to submit to the community, which would include the state. Right before Paul gave instructions on marriage he instructed believers to "Submit to **one another** out of reverence for Christ" (Ephesians 5:21-33).

Another glaring reason to make one's marriage legal is that marriage is **the defining point** of fornication, adultery and divorce:

1. **Fornication** is sex before marriage
2. **Adultery** is sex outside of one's marriage
3. **Divorce** is the dissolution of marriage

When it's not clear who is married and who is not married it leads to moral ambiguity and the corresponding lawlessness.

Is a "Common Law Marriage" Acceptable for Believers?

A common law marriage is a marriage wherein a couple agrees to cohabitate as committed man & wife without a civil or religious ceremony, which should be distinguished from whimsically living together in fornication with no intent of commitment. **The Lord distinguishes the two and cannot be fooled** (John 4:16-18).

Common law marriage is acceptable for believers in situations where there is no access to legal marriage, like if they're stuck on a deserted island. The case of Isaac & Rebecca, noted above, is another example, but in their situation there was no state to acknowledge their marriage, although it was acknowledged by their families.

In modern day nations, however, there's no reason *not* to make one's marriage clear to society by making it legally binding. Even in cases where the state acknowledges common law marriages, believers should make their marital union more concrete for appearances sake so as not to be a bad witness, as already noted.

But let's say the couple doesn't want to get legally married because their taxes will go up or the woman will lose government assistance if she documents herself as married. If the couple does this, they are *lying* about their marital status to the government for reasons of monetary gain (greed).

This obviously would not be a case of justifiable lying, as when the Hebrew midwives lied to Pharaoh to save the lives of male babies (Exodus 1:15-21) or when Rahab lied to the king of Jericho to save the Hebrew spies (Joshua 2:1-6 & James 2:25). No matter how you slice it, it's a shaky foundation on which to set a marriage, not to mention it reflects lack of faith in God's provision for their new life together.

In situations where a couple rejects the traditional concept of a wedding — whether pronounced by a minister or a judge — and only have a relationship within the commitment of common law marriage, they are fully bound in marriage together. In other words, they are indeed married. *But* they have an issue with rebellion — bucking the system, thinking that they are above the law, disrespecting customs and traditions of their culture, dishonoring their families and community.

Yes, they are married. But what about submitting their matrimony to the fellowship of the community and the authority of the state? Submission is not a popular subject because the flesh doesn't like to acknowledge or submit to someone else's power. But submitting to one another and the governing authorities — physical and spiritual — is a Christ-like trait (Ephesians 5:21, 1 Peter 5:5 & Romans 13:1-6). So this is an issue of pride, not a marriage issue. Believing men & women who decide to be married *should* do the paperwork.

There's another obvious problem with couples who refuse to make their marriage more binding through a ceremony & legal documentation: It smacks of "leaving the door open" in case their relationship doesn't work out, which makes it easier to bail when difficulties inevitably arise. If either spouse chooses to abandon the relationship they have a readymade excuse: "Well, we weren't *technically* married."

That said, there may be unique situations where it would be wise for a married couple to keep mum about their marriage, like in Nazi Germany if a German citizen married a Jew. In these types of circumstances couples have to be led of the Holy Spirit.

Weddings are Rites of Passage

While Isaac & Rebecca didn't have much of a wedding ceremony (Genesis 24:67), we know more elaborate ceremonies occurred because Christ's first miracle took place at a wedding celebration in Cana (John 2:1-11).

Meanwhile the idea of a written contract can be found in the apocryphal book of Tobit:

> **Then Raguel summoned his daughter Sarah. When she came to him he took her by the hand and gave her to Tobias, saying, 'Take her to be your wife in accordance with the law and decree written in the book of Moses. Take her and bring her safely to your father. And may the God of heaven prosper your journey with his peace.' 13 Then he called her mother and told her to bring writing material; and he wrote out a copy of a marriage contract, to the effect that he gave her to him as wife according to the decree of the law of Moses. 14 Then they began to eat and drink.**
>
> **Tobit 7:12-14** (NRSVA)

This simple "ceremony" consisted of the father handing his daughter over to the groom with his blessing and writing a contract regarding the family agreement, which was documented proof of their marriage. Is this not basically what takes place in weddings today?

While this is an apocryphal passage, it nevertheless shows that marriages were legitimized via written documentation in the 8th

Century BC, which is when the events of the book take place (721 BC). The book itself, however, was written somewhere between 225-175 BC, which means that Tobit shows that written marriage contracts can be traced back *at least* to the 3rd Century, BC.

Whether the ceremony is elaborate like the wedding banquet at Cana or simple like this one or Isaac & Rebecca's union (Genesis 24:67), it's not the formality that makes the marriage real, but rather the intent and design of the bride and groom's heart. Even in the event that a man & woman who decide to marry are stuck on a deserted island they would certainly have some kind of rite wherein they agreed to be married and thus committed to one another for life. For instance, enslaved people in the 1800s couldn't legally marry, but that didn't stop them from having a "jumping the broom" ceremony.

Whether elaborate or simple, the ceremony is a rite of passage wherein the reality of their new status is established and then commemorated in years to come. The couple and their community view this event — this date — as a turning point in their life journey, separating their prior singleness from their ongoing unity as "one flesh."

I should add that the written contract does not make a marriage reality. The son of a friend of mine got married a few years ago in a state where you are required to have the minister — or whoever the officiator is — sign the marriage license application and then return the paper work to the county clerk; in a few weeks you'd receive the legal marriage certificate. Yet the couple went on their honeymoon the next morning and completely forgot about doing the paperwork until almost a year later when they finally got it straight.

Does this mean they weren't married for nine months? Were they "living in sin" for that period of time? Of course not. They were married the day they agreed to be united in holy matrimony. The written document has to do with the government legally acknowledging the marriage that already existed.

I remember a couple of old movie stars, like Kirk Douglas, making statements that they didn't believe men can be monogamous. But this is a scapegoat to commit adultery or live in fornication. It explains *why* the bride & groom **vow** to be faithful to one another. In other words, yes, humans — and especially males — have a predilection for successive romantic/sexual partners and this is precisely *why* it's necessary for married couples to **vow** to be committed to one another till death do them part.

Why Loyalty is Important

To be faithful is to be loyal. In other words, faithfulness *is* loyalty. It's a fruit of the spirit and therefore the opposite of a work of the flesh (Galatians 5:19-23).

Loyalty is underrated these days. Honor the one who wears your ring. Write loyalty on the tablet of your heart (Proverbs 3:3) and your marriage will last, assuming your partner feels the same way. Speaking of which...

When looking for a spouse, loyalty should be high up on your list of preferences since it is one of the most priceless qualities for a secure, happy marriage. Perhaps the worst thing for a husband or wife to experience is an impenitent unfaithful spouse. Unfortunately it's relatively common in this ignoble age.

What's the Purpose of Marriage?

So the scriptural definition of marriage is: A man & a woman *agreeing* to be united as man & wife, "one flesh," as long as they live (Genesis 2:24). But what is God's *reason* for marriage? Simple: Social chaos would result from unbridled or casual pairings seeing as how the strategic underpinning that the family unit offers society would disintegrate.

In other words, God set up the lifetime commitment of husband & wife — the marital covenant — as the firm base for a healthy society. Show me a community where the family unit breaks down or is nonexistent due to fornication, unfaithfulness and so on and I'll show you a lawless society with many glaring problems.

Just as important, the LORD instituted marriage as the means in which a man and a woman become "one flesh" in its fullest and most satisfying sense. Casual sex may have its allure, not to mention temporary fleshly gratification, but it results in death in one form or another since "the wages of sin is death" (Romans 6:23). Nothing beats the ongoing joy and peace of a healthy marriage and family!

What about Polygamy?

It was noted in chapter **4** that, while God *permitted* Israelite men to marry several wives, polygamy is *not* the Creator's ideal for marriage, as plainly observed in the beginning (Matthew 19:4-6). Polygamous marriages chronicled in God's Word suffered conflict with the predictable jealousy of the wives, such as Rachel and Leah in Genesis 29:31-30:24.

In the New Testament era leaders in the Church are instructed to have but one spouse (1 Timothy 3:2, 3:12 & Titus 1:6), which was to be an ***example*** to the Christians in their midst (1 Timothy 4:12 & 1 Peter 5:3). So, while the New Covenant Scriptures don't exactly prohibit polygamy, they definitely encourage the LORD's ideal as established in Genesis — one husband, one wife, till death do them part.

But why did God permit polygamy in ancient times? Here are a couple of likely reasons:

- The world at the time generally consisted of patriarchal societies where females relied on their fathers, brothers and husbands for provision & protection. Thus marriage, even if it was polygamous, protected women from a life of poverty, prostitution or slavery.
- Polygamy also facilitated God's Genesis directive to "be fruitful and multiply, and fill the earth" (Genesis 1:28, 9:1 & 9:7) seeing as how husbands could impregnate other wives while one was pregnant/giving birth. This allowed men to have several children per year, as opposed to just one, and this was conducive to the increase & spread of humanity on the planet.

What about Divorce?

The Bible's definition of marriage shows that it's meant to last until one of the spouses dies. "God hates divorce," the Scriptures say (Malachi 2:16). The Mosaic Law only permitted divorce because of the hardness of the Hebrews' hearts (Matthew 19:8).

That said, Christ acknowledged that unfaithfulness is grounds for divorce (Matthew 5:32, 19:9 & Luke 16:18). However, if the guilty spouse is genuinely repentant I encourage working it out and persevering. In other words, while divorcing due to unfaithfulness is permissible, it's not mandated. At the end of the day, though, it's up to the offended spouse in question and the leading of the Spirit.

Further grounds for divorce would be abandonment or impenitent abuse:

> **But if the unbeliever leaves, let it be so. The brother or the sister is not bound in such circumstances; God has called us to live in peace.**
> **1 Corinthians 7:15**

Concerning abuse, the verse stresses that "God has called us **to live in peace" in relation to the marriage covenant**. Obviously this divine calling *cannot* be accomplished or maintained if one of the spouses is seriously abusive and unrepentant about it.

Every individual is unique and every marital situation is distinctive. So I always encourage seeking the Lord on what to do when your spouse is unfaithful or wickedly abusive. Obviously if the offender is stubbornly impenitent the marriage will not work out. As it is written, "Can two walk together, unless they are agreed?" (Amos 3:3 NKJV).

An unloved woman who is married is such a perversion of reality — the way it's *supposed* to be — that it figuratively shakes the planet:

> **21 Under three things the earth trembles,**
> **under four it cannot bear up:**
> **22 a servant who becomes king,**
> **a fool who is full of food,**
> **23 an unloved woman who is married,**

and a maidservant who displaces her mistress.

Proverbs 30:21-23

In other words, an unloved or abused wife is an abomination according to the Bible.

At the end of the day believers are to be led of the Spirit (Romans 8:14) and do what they have a peace about doing (Colossians 3:15 & Philippians 4:7).

What about Remarriage?

If an individual divorces for one of the legitimate reasons noted above, s/he can remain single, which has its benefits according to Scripture (1 Corinthians 7:7,28,32-34), or remarry if led of the Spirit to do so. Obviously you don't want to make rash decisions about marrying an individual.

My wife, Carol, divorced her former husband on the grounds of unfaithfulness. The fact that he was a pathological liar didn't help matters. Led of the Spirit, we married and have been one-flesh for 27 years as of this writing.

If someone divorces for biblically *illegitimate* reasons they'll have to work it out with the LORD as far as staying single, re-marrying their former spouse or possibly marrying someone else. It's between them and their Maker. Do what you have the faith to do (Romans 14:23 & Titus 1:15). Divorcing for illegitimate reasons is a sin, but nowhere does Scripture say that divorce is an *unforgiveable* offense. As with any transgression, the LORD will forgive us when we humbly confess (1 John 1:8-9) and God casts the sin into the sea of forgetfulness (Micah 7:19). Then you move on guided by the Spirit.

Anyone — including Christian servant-leaders — who imply that they *never* sin is a **liar** (Proverbs 20:9, Ecclesiastes 7:20 & 1 John 1:8).

Should a Believer Marry an Unbeliever?

No. If a believer does this s/he will automatically get the devil as a father-in-law (John 8:44 & 1 John 3:10) and the couple will be unequally yoked (2 Corinthians 6:14).

That said, if a believer *does* foolishly marry an unbeliever there's always hope for the situation with the LORD involved (Psalm 71:14 & 130:7). We serve a God of miracles who can do *anything* in response to simple faith (Jeremiah 32:27 & Mark 9:23)!

In cases where one of the spouses of an *already-married* couple gets saved, the Scriptures instruct the believer to continue in the marriage unless the unbelieving spouse decides to abandon the union (1 Corinthians 7:15). Obviously the other two legitimate grounds for divorce noted earlier apply as well.

Additional Thoughts on the Purpose of Marriage

We already looked at the purpose of marriage, but it's worth considering again with some further insights…

The marriage covenant between a man & woman has several purposes: intimate fellowship with another soul — spiritually, mentally and physically (Matthew 19:4-6); procreation; a legitimate outlet for sexual activity and the corresponding pleasure (Proverbs 5:18-19); preventing the spread of immorality and the corresponding sexual diseases (1 Corinthians 7:2); and providing a strategic foundational sanctuary for children wherein they are lovingly brought up in the training and instruction of the Lord (Ephesians 6:4).

Yet there's a deeper purpose as marriage is actually a type of God's relationship with the redeemed (Ephesians 5:31–32). This is mind-blowing: The Church is the "bride of Christ" and we will collectively be married to the Lord in eternity (2 Corinthians 11:2 & Revelation 19:7-9). We'll look at this fascinating truth further in the **Epilogue**.

New Testament Instructions for Married Couples

Here's what Paul instructed married couples by the Holy Spirit:

> **Submit to one another out of reverence for Christ.**
> **22 Wives, submit yourselves to your own husbands as you do to the Lord. 23 For the husband is the head of the wife as Christ is the head of the church, his body, of which he is the Savior. 24 Now as the church submits to Christ, so also wives should submit to their husbands in everything.**
> **25 Husbands, love your wives, just as Christ loved the church and gave himself up for her 26 to make her holy, cleansing her by the washing with water through the word, 27 and to present her to himself as a radiant church, without stain or wrinkle or any other blemish, but holy and**

> **blameless. [28] In this same way, husbands ought to**
> **love their wives as their own bodies. He who**
> **loves his wife loves himself. [29] After all, no one**
> **ever hated their own body, but they feed and**
> **care for their body, just as Christ does the**
> **church— [30] for we are members of his body.**
> **[31]“For this reason a man will leave his father and**
> **mother and be united to his wife, and the two**
> **will become one flesh.” [32] This is a profound**
> **mystery—but I am talking about Christ and the**
> **church. [33] However, each one of you also must**
> **love his wife as he loves himself, and the wife**
> **must respect her husband.**
>
> **Ephesians 5:21-33**

Any important decision in marriage should obviously be prayed about and discussed by the couple; then they should do what they *agree* to do since they’re “one flesh.” Interestingly, Abraham was the progenitor of the Hebrews and the “father of faith” (Romans 3:27-4:25) yet it was his wife, Sarah, who made the decision to acquire Hagar so Abraham could have children through her since Sarah couldn’t bear offspring at the time (Genesis 16). It was also her decision to exile Hagar & Ishmael (the latter being Abraham & Hagar’s child) after she became jealous.

My point is that **Abraham complied with both decisions** (Genesis 21). However, one of the spouses has to have the final say on a matter in cases of disagreement and that is, according to the Scriptures, the husband since he is the “head.”

You’ll note in the Ephesians passage that the husband’s headship isn’t an excuse for abuse. In fact the text **exhorts husbands to love their wives *three times*…**

1. in a self-sacrificial manner as Christ loves the Church (verse 25);
2. as their own bodies (verse 28); and
3. as themselves (verse 33).

Why should husbands love their wives "*as* their own bodies" – "*as* themselves"? Because **a married couple is not two, but one**. As such, what you do to your spouse, you do to yourself. Thus wives are instructed to respect their husband; if they don't, they're disrespecting *themselves*.

What's the Secret of a Successful Marriage?

The Bible says that "a cord of three strands is not quickly broken" (Ecclesiastes 4:12). In a marriage the three-strand cord consists of **husband**, **wife** and the **LORD**. As the husband and wife draw nearer to the Lord (James 4:8), they naturally come nearer to each other, as illustrated here:

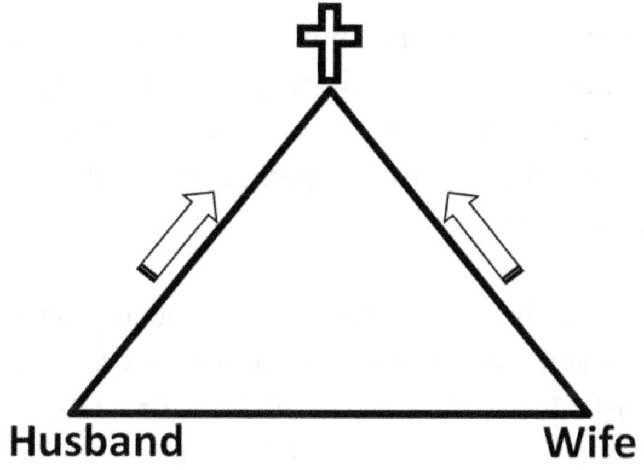

Closing Thoughts

The goal of this chapter was to provide general scriptural instructions on marriage and related topics. The main purpose is to understand the *biblical* definition of marriage, which is a covenant — an agreement — of a committed relationship between a biological male & female, which doesn't require a pronouncement by an official, whether a minister or judge, nor does it demand a written document for verification.

This should help the Church relate to and serve couples who — for whatever reason — haven't (yet) made their marriages more legally binding in a conventional sense. This is not to suggest, of course, that every couple who's living together is married; many are just living in fornication until they choose to leave at whim, which obviously is *not* marriage and the Lord *knows* this (John 4:16-18).

For *believers,* it's wise to make our marriages legally-binding for the reasons noted, including respect & submission to the community and corresponding authorities, which makes for a good Christian witness. This explains why a pastor might counsel a Common Law-married couple to make their marriage more legally binding by doing the paperwork, particularly if they want to join the assembly in question.

Beyond that, we should be careful about nosing into a couple's marital details and simply take them at their word; after all, that's what the LORD does (Matthew 12:36-37 & Proverbs 18:21). Such things are between them and their Maker. Let the Word of God and the Holy Spirit guide them, convict them, etc.

12

Why You Shouldn't Put Men or Women in a Box, Marriages too

Please be careful to *not* put people in a box, either gender; and this includes marriages.

For instance, Jacob was renamed Israel and became the progenitor of God's nation on Earth, but he was a Momma's boy who favored hanging around the tents while his half-brother, Esau, was a hairy manly man who preferred the outdoors and hunting (Genesis 25:27, 27:11 & 27:22-23). In short, Jacob was stereotypically Liberal whereas Esau was stereotypically Rightwing. Obviously God had no problem using a so-called "Momma's boy" as an instrumental figure in the divine plan for humanity's redemption.

In the New Testament Christ reveals his loving gentleness at times (Matthew 11:29) — a supposedly Liberal trait — while at other times he was a veritable holy terror (Mark 11:15-18). As Solomon said, "It is good to grasp the one and not let go of the other.

Whoever fears God will avoid all extremes" (Ecclesiastes 7:16-18).

Meanwhile the Lord pointed out the glaring contrasts of those who live off the grid in the wilderness compared to the well-to-do in the city: John the Baptist wore garments made of camel hair and ate locusts & wild honey while those who live in palaces wear fine apparel and dine on exquisite cuisines (Matthew 3:1-6 & 11:7-8).

Regarding women, the Bible features the all-encompassing national leadership of Deborah for four decades (Judges 4:4-9) as well as the meek purity of Mother Mary (Luke 1:26-56). Then there's mighty Jael *(yah-AYL)* who had no qualms about smashing a tent peg through the temple of a Canaanite commander (Judges 4:17-22). Meanwhile sisters Martha & Mary were like night and day (Luke 10:38-42).

As far as marriages go, they all feature different dynamics based on two unique people and their corresponding social stratum. In today's society, women aren't necessarily preoccupied with raising kids for about 30 years from the start of their early marriages, as was normally the case in biblical times. They may likely work outside the home and have careers while husbands may have unconventional occupations, working from or at the home.

Furthermore, the couple's ages might not match what is conventional. For instance, the wife might be older than the husband. So what?

Allow Christian couples to make their own decisions about these matters and who does what or why, working within scriptural guidelines as led of the Holy Spirit. Don't nose into other people's business. How God works in other believers' lives is none of your or my concern; our concern is to follow the Lord and fulfill the responsibilities of our distinctive callings (John 21:21-22).

Paul expressed it perfectly when he asked, “Who are you to judge someone else’s servant?” (Romans 14:4). He was referring to judging other believers on any type of non-essential, disputable matter, like what food to eat and what holiday to celebrate. By stressing “someone else’s servant,” Paul meant God’s servant, that is, other believers. Simply put, other believers are *God’s* servant, not your servant or my servant.

Even in cases where a believer functions within a pastor’s “flock,” the pastor is merely the *under*-shepherd, not the Chief Shepherd; Christ is the Chief Shepherd (1 Peter 5:1-4). This is why the text instructs pastors to not lord it over believers, but rather be humble, godly examples (if they can’t do that then they have no business being pastors).

13

Is Oral Sex Okay?

I'm addressing this tricky question because someone wrote me wanting an honest answer based on scriptural truth. If one person is asking this question, others are too (they just prefer to remain silent because it's a TMI sort of topic).

The Bible doesn't specifically mention oral sex, but arguably implies it in a figurative sense in the Song of Songs. As covered in **Part I**, this poetic book features sensuous lyrics filled with suggestive imagery that applauds sexuality as a normal part of marital life between a biological man and woman. Obviously sexual activity outside of the marriage covenant is not sanctioned by the LORD.

Here's an example of what I'm talking about with the woman in the song speaking about her man:

> **3 Like an apple tree among the trees of the forest**
> **is my beloved among the young men.**
> **I delight to sit in his shade,**
> **and his fruit is sweet to my taste.**
> **4 Let him lead me to the banquet hall,**

and let his banner over me be love.
5 Strengthen me with raisins,
refresh me with apples,
for I am faint with love.
6 His left arm is under my head,
and his right arm embraces me.

Song of Songs 2:3-6

While the woman is likely engaging in fantasy in this exchange, as pointed out in chapter 5, it doesn't negate what the words suggest.

And here's an example of the man speaking of the one his heart desires:

6 How beautiful you are and how pleasing,
my love, with your delights!
7 Your stature is like that of the palm,
and your breasts like clusters of fruit.
8 I said, "I will climb the palm tree;
I will take hold of its fruit."
May your breasts be like clusters of grapes on the vine,
the fragrance of your breath like apples,
9 and your mouth like the best wine.

Song of Songs 7:6-9

This is presumably Solomon flattering the lovely maiden he desires (and she rejects him for her humble shepherd, according to the three-character interpretation).

In any case, there are Christians who find such frank romantic sensuality in the Bible surprising, which compels some religionists to interpret the passages in a strictly symbolic sense relating to God's love for Israel or Christ's love for his "bride," the Church.

While I've no doubt that these verses can be interpreted on such a level, it doesn't change the fact that we must first regard them from a purely straightforward standpoint.

So can spouses partake of oral sex with their mates or not? It's entirely up to the individual and what they believe. If the husband & wife have no qualms, what's it to me? If they do have qualms or simply don't want to do it, then obviously they shouldn't. The Bible puts it like this: "everything that does not come from faith [belief] is sin" (Romans 14:23). The Scriptures also say "**To the pure, all things are pure**, but to those who are corrupted and do not believe, nothing is pure" (Titus 1:15).

At the end of the day it's a private issue between husbands & wives.

14

An Honest Look at the 'M' Word (Masturbation)

I debated on whether or not to include this chapter because the Song of Songs is such a beautiful book of the Bible that tastefully addresses delicate topics of romantic love, marriage and sex. I simply didn't want to mar it with a subject that is — let's face it — so private, so intimate, it's understandably awkward to openly discuss, even embarrassing.

While I decided to included it for reasons explained at the end of this chapter, I must emphasize: If you can't handle an honest examination of this very personal, adult-oriented issue, I suggest skipping it and maybe coming back later.

Introduction

Back in the '80s an Evangelical pastor who was popular with young people spoke frankly on the topic of masturbation and tried to be balanced. Being a controversial topic, interviewers would naturally ask him about it. He responded, "Look, I'll answer your questions to the best of my knowledge and understanding, but I don't want to be known as the 'masturbation pastor'; that's not where my heart is." I feel the same here.

The two extreme positions on the issue reflect the Conservative and Liberal mindsets. It's wise to consider the evidence for both sides, along with the Middle Ground position, before drawing plausible conclusions that apply to one's own situation. That's what we're going to do here.

Let's start with the fact that…

The Bible Doesn't Directly Mention Masturbation

Whatever answers we come up with in this chapter, they will be from indirect material since the topic of masturbation is not mentioned in the Holy Scriptures. In short, there's no commandment "Thou Shalt Not Masturbate." Sexual lust is detailed, of course, but not self-stimulation of the genitals for gratification.

For anyone who might cite Onan from Genesis 38:8-10, this man's offense was not masturbation, but rather the refusal to fulfill his Hebraic duty in perpetuating his brother's line of descendants (Deuteronomy 25:5-10).

The obvious question is: Why *doesn't* the Creator mention masturbation in the God-breathed Scriptures — the LORD's written Word to humanity (2 Timothy 3:16-17) — a topic that practically every human being has to deal with during his/her life on Earth? Perhaps because it's not a cut-and-dried issue and, whether or not masturbation is a sin, depends on several things, which will be detailed as we progress.

As such, each individual will have to work out this private issue in his/her personal relationship with their Creator with fear and trembling (Philippians 2:12).

That said, I want to stress that…

A Person is a Slave to Whatever Has Mastered Him/Her

Peter put it like this:

> **They promise them freedom, while they themselves are slaves of depravity—for "people are slaves to whatever has mastered them."**
>
> **2 Peter 2:19**

If a person allows himself/herself to become in bondage to something that's not necessary for survival (water, food, air, etc.) they in essence become a slave to that thing, not to mention the thing in question becomes a figurative idol.

Christianity is all about true freedom, which includes freedom *from* the flesh and religious legalism (2 Corinthians 3:17 & Galatians 5:1), but it also supports the wisdom of moderation in all things so as not to be hindered or mastered by anything (Hebrews 12:1 & 1 Corinthians 6:12).

Anything that impedes a person's productivity in life automatically becomes a destructive "weight" and needs to be "thrown off." This would include the practice of masturbation. Such things must be understood at the outset of this study along with the fact that…

Believers Are Instructed to Control Their Bodies

This can be observed in Paul's instruction to the Thessalonians:

> **It is God's will that you should be sanctified: that you should avoid sexual immorality; [4] that each of you should learn to control your own body in a way that is holy and honorable, [5] not in passionate lust like the pagans, who do not know God; [6] and that in this matter no one should wrong or take advantage of a brother or sister. The Lord will punish all those who commit such sins, as we told you and warned you before. [7] For God did not call us to be impure, but to live a holy life.**
>
> **1 Thessalonians 4:3-7**

Verse 5 reveals that the issue comes down to knowing God or not knowing God. The spiritually-regenerated believer who walks with the Lord is expected to control his/her body in a way that is holy and honorable, not in passionate lust like unbelievers who aren't walking with the Lord.

This shows that the Creator wants his children to be in a **state of control** over their bodies & thoughts/actions and not in bondage to anything. Yet verse 4 plainly says that believers have to "learn" to control their bodies; in other words, it's a *process* — there is a *progression* that goes with sanctification (1 Thessalonians 5:23).

Secondly, while the text is pretty straightforward, there's also a degree of mystery: What exactly does "control your body in a way that is holy and honorable, not in passionate lust" mean for each individual? Obviously the indwelling Spirit is going to have to guide & help each believer in this matter. The Spirit's guidance will depend on the maturity level of the person, their unique situation and their calling. Such things will be elucidated as we continue.

Now let's consider the three perspectives on masturbation and the pros or cons of each (keeping in mind that there are variations among these three).

The Conservative View: Masturbation is Always a Sin

This is the go-to position for many Evangelicals, which makes masturbation a black & white issue. They base it on the fact that Christ said, "But I tell you that anyone who looks at a woman lustfully has already committed adultery with her in his heart" (Matthew 5:28), which is bolstered by righteous Job's attitude: "I made a covenant with my eyes not to look lustfully at a young woman" (Job 31:1) and similar comments made in verses 9-12.

These passages support the obvious connection between what goes on in the mind to one's potential actions (as well as the error of objectifying a woman due to her physical beauty). And, since it's arguably impossible to masturbate without the use of imagination, advocates of this position reason that masturbation is always a sin.

Until the individual is married, they reason, the sexual side of life can be totally shut down through walking in the spirit (Ephesians 4:22-24). Of course learning to live by the Spirit is a process and so the believer will have to "keep with repentance" when they inevitably miss it (Matthew 3:8 & 1 John 1:8-9).

Speaking of marriage, supporters of this view point to God's original design for the two genders, male & female, to unite together in marriage and multiply (Genesis 2:18 & 1:28) — with nothing being said about masturbation in the Song of Songs, which is God's poetic 'manual' on romantic love/sex/marriage.

Likewise, the New Testament says zilch about masturbation when the topics of singlehood and marriage surface. For instance, the apostle Paul argued that, since sexual immorality abounds, "each man should have sexual relations with his own wife, and each woman with her own husband" (1 Corinthians 7:2). While Paul stressed the positive points of being single, particularly in that time and place (Corinth, a city about 50 miles west of Athens, Greece), he also pointed out that marriage is the natural solution for the single person who can't control himself/herself for "it is better to marry than to burn with passion" (1 Corinthians 7:9). This would be the fitting place for Paul, led of the Spirit, to bring up the topic of masturbation, but he mysteriously says nada.

Is nothing said about masturbation in these key passages because it's implied that it's a prohibited, sinful practice, as supporters of this position would argue, or is it simply because God leaves the issue open for each individual to work out in his/her relationship with the LORD? (Philippians 2:12).

As far as releasing pent-up sexual energy goes, adherents of this view maintain that the Creator has provided a natural way for a person to release constrained sexuality; it's called the "wet dream" (Deuteronomy 23:10-11). As such, masturbation is not necessary to release bottled-up sexual energy since a "nocturnal emission" will naturally do it for the individual.

If you are satisfied with the arguments for this position, I encourage you to stick with it (Romans 14:14). However, if you discern some holes or unexplained details, read on. But, first, let's consider the other side of the spectrum…

The Liberal View: Masturbation is Not a Sin

A moderate Liberal argued that masturbation was God's gift to assist people with pent-up sexual energy (presumably single people). While this sounds somewhat reasonable, the radical Liberal position goes back to the sexual revolution of the '60s and the foolish Leftie mantra: *"If it feels good do it."* This is the philosophy of hedonism. Those who subscribe to hedonism are libertines.

When it comes to carnal desires, no matter how questionable, libertines typically encourage the embracing of the whim. After all, you were "born that way," they argue, and so you are free to indulge because "it's the way you were made."

Does this mean a 45 year-old male is free to pursue having sex with a 14 year-old girl because he experiences the desire and therefore was "born that way"? Should a woman who has the whim to eat 2 gallons of ice cream per day do so because she was "born that way"? Should a youth become a druggie/drunkard because he has the desire to be wasted? Obviously not in all three cases. This reveals the absurdity of libertinism: Just because you experience a desire doesn't automatically mean it's good and you should act on it or base your life around it.

Speaking of which, Liberals tend to encourage people to base their identities around curious desires and whims. To deny a flesh urge is repression to them; and repression of desire, they reason, creates a "repressed" individual, which they consider mental illness. Personal discipline is an abomination to libertines unless it involves things like performing yoga or not using straws. Yes, I'm being amusing, but it's pretty much the truth when it comes to Leftwing people.

It comes as no surprise, therefore, that the Liberal view on masturbation is that it's natural & healthy and can be practiced as often as the individual wishes, regardless of whether he/she is single or married. It's in line with their motto *"If it feels good, do it!"*

Since modern-day Liberalism is equal to what the Bible calls "the world" (1 John 2:15-17) — and explains why I refer to it as **LIE**beralism — this viewpoint can be dismissed out of hand in this discussion. Remember, these are the folks who say with a straight face that there are 152 genders (or whatever the tally is these days) and that a man can become a woman by simply having his penis surgically removed whereupon he can legitimately compete in female competitions and be praised for winning.

The Middle Ground: Masturbation May or May Not be a Sin, Depending on the Individual and Details Thereof

This view argues that, since masturbation is not mentioned in the Bible and there is no direct prohibition against it, whether or not it is permissible in a person's life depends on his/her unique position, their level of spiritual maturity and the leading of the Spirit. Let's look at each of these:

- **The person's unique position:** God doesn't make people 'cookie-cutter'; we're all unique. What may be an issue for one person is not an issue whatsoever for another. For instance, Paul spoke of his gift of sexual continence to which he acknowledged many others don't have, yet they have other gifts (1 Corinthians 7:7). Some single men have exceptionally high sex drives and the occasional 'wet dream' arguably isn't going to cut it for them. As for Paul's argument that "it is better to marry than to burn with passion" (1 Corinthians 7:9), while this may be true, it would be extremely foolish to marry someone solely on the grounds of sexual gratification since it's a huge commitment and life-altering matter. To say nothing of it involving the life of another human being.

- **The person's level of spiritual maturity:** There's a world of difference between, say, a new believer at 20 years of age and a seasoned man or woman of God of 55. There are stages to spiritual growth, not to mention keys to spiritual development (2 Peter 1:2-11), and so everyone isn't at the same place.
- **Conscience and the leading of the Spirit in the individual's life:** Since masturbation isn't mentioned in the Scriptures and there is no direct prohibition against it, the believer is going to have to go by the leading of the Spirit within and the conviction thereof (1 John 3:19-24). In other words, if your conscience & indwelling Spirit convict you of something, then don't do it. If there is no conviction — at least currently — then you can be certain that "to the pure all things are pure" (Titus 1:15). However, when the Spirit guides you to remove something from your life, you are obligated to do so since "you are not your own, you were bought at a price" (1 Corinthians 6:19-20).

It goes without saying that we have to be careful with the verse that says "to the pure all things are pure." This shouldn't be mistaken to mean that a sin can ever be pure, like adultery. We also have to be careful of the self-deception of being "pure in our own eyes" (Proverbs 16:2 & Proverbs 30:12).

While the Middle Ground position respects the Conservative view and admits that believers should stick with that position if they're convinced of it, à la Romans 14:14, it objects to its black & white simplicity. For instance, both Matthew 5:28 and Job 3:1 are talking about committing *adultery* within one's heart. But what if a married man is away from home for a long period of time and releases his sexual energy by masturbating to thoughts of his wife? By doing this, he reasons, he'll be less prone to amorous temptations on the road. Obviously this wouldn't be adultery and the masturbation would arguably be permissible.

For those who understandably contend that the same principle would apply to the sin of fornication, what if the 'woman' in question is a drawing or image. To explain, in concentration camps, like Soviet gulags, artists would draw an alluring sketch of a woman and barter it to other captives. How exactly can a man commit fornication with a 'woman' that doesn't exist? In other words, if what the person is imagining when he/she masturbates involves an unreal figure, how exactly is it a sin, unless of course the Spirit leads that person to not do it or stop the practice?

What if a single man with an exceptional sex drive expunges his sexual energy in this manner on the grounds that it will assist in evading amorous temptations, including the allure of porn, which is always just a click away in the modern day? In other words, to him, it basically removes that challenge from the table and frees him up for spiritual things. I'm not necessarily agreeing with this position, just sharing what guys have said who deal with this real-life issue.

On top of all this is the glaring question: When does merely appreciating beauty end and sinister lust begin?

These kinds of questions are naturally troubling to those who see everything in black & white, which is what some believers in STAGE TWO tend to do. STAGE TWO, if you're not familiar with the four stages of spiritual growth, is the childhood stage of spiritual development (1 John 2:9-14).[8] This is said with zero condescension; it's simply a reflection of the way it is with spiritual growth and non-growth. Yet we're talking real-life issues and struggles here, which demand frankness and tackling the hard questions.

In any case, the Middle Ground position acknowledges that masturbation is something that the Lord will eventually weed out of a person's life as he/she grows, à la Colossians 3:5 and 1 Thessalonians 4:3-7, but this is going to be accomplished by the Spirit's leading and not some legalistic religious rule that's not actually cited in the Bible. It's the aforementioned *process of* sanctification.

Remember, the Bible emphasizes God's compassion, which means **sympathetic understanding** of our plight in this fallen world (Psalm 145:9 & Hebrews 4:15). In short, anyone struggling with the things we're talking about here, the Lord *understands* — the Lord *cares*. God's not some ogre in the sky just itching to smash people with a cosmic club; the Lord's full of love, mercy and compassion for his children (Psalm 86:15, 103:8 & 103:13), which is *not* to say that that there isn't a time for divine discipline (Hebrews 12:5-7). God is for you, not against you (Romans 8:31). It's of the utmost importance to your spiritual health that you get a hold of this.

---

[8] The Bible plainly acknowledges levels of spiritual development with phrases like going "from strength to strength" or "glory to glory" (Psalm 84:5,7 & 2 Corinthians 3:18). Yet 1 John 2:9-14 specifically cites four main levels: **darkness**, **childhood**, **youth** and **maturity**. For details see the article *Spiritual Growth — The Four Stages* at the FOL site or pick up a copy of my book *The Four Stages of Spiritual Growth*.

A young minister strongly advocated the Conservative position in an honest article, arguing that masturbation is indeed a sin, yet the reason for his rigid stance was revealed in his testimony: He became captive to the practice in his teens and desperately wanted freedom. Upon turning to the Lord he acquired emancipation, but the experience unsurprisingly left him viewing masturbation as a great sin and his personal #1 flesh-enemy.

Yet this doesn't necessarily make masturbation a sin any more than it makes playing computer games a sin because an individual is in bondage to the activity. What about the gazillions of people who play computer games, but they do so in moderation and there's zero bondage?

The same goes for the severe alcoholic who turns to the Lord and escapes the bondage of drunkard-ness. Just because drinking alcohol is a sin to this person, it doesn't mean another person who isn't an alcoholic can't drink a sip of alcohol now and then, assuming s/he is in an environment that's not going to make someone stumble (Romans 14:13-23). Are you following?

I shared at the end of chapter **9** how one pastor I served under adamantly taught from the pulpit that merely shopping at a store that sells alcoholic beverages is a sin. Why? Not because the Bible says it's a sin, obviously, but rather because he was a serious alcoholic before giving his life to the Lord and this caused him to unjustly condemn *anything* involving alcoholic beverages, even if it wasn't immoral from a biblical standpoint. (While this is wrong and grossly legalistic, the Holy Spirit *might* of course lead a specific believer to *not* shop at a certain establishment for one reason or another).

Speaking of alcoholic beverages, supporters of the Middle Ground position believe masturbation could be equated to the topic of alcohol in the Bible. While being a drunkard is indeed a sin (Galatians 5:19-21), drinking in moderation is not (Matthew 11:19 & 1 Timothy 5:23) — assuming a believer even chooses to drink an alcoholic beverage in the first place (some could care less about alcohol, like me).

As long as it doesn't compel anyone who struggles with alcoholism to fall or troubles someone with a weak conscience, it's allowable. In short, just as drinking alcohol can become a bondage and therefore detrimental to someone's life, so can masturbation, yet neither are evil in-and-of-themselves (Romans 14:14). The details of the person, their situation and the leading of the Spirit will determine if either is permissible or destructive at the time.

Concluding Thoughts

I was reluctant to include this chapter because the topic is controversial and any minister who doesn't staunchly support the Conservative position is readily written off as "going Liberal" (at least in Evangelical circles). But that's hardly the case here. In any event, there's pressure for ministers to tout the Evangelical convention on this topic — the Conservative position — or just keep mum on the subject.

Since masturbation is not directly mentioned in Scripture — and God obviously did this intentionally — it comes down to a matter between the individual believer and their Creator. It's one of those "disputable" issues that should be kept between the person and their LORD (Romans 14:22) as they weigh the applicable verses of Scripture, their conscience and the guidance of the Spirit. In short, **it's a *private* matter**.

Someone mocked to me the idea of God — the Creator of all things — caring about what a guy does with his pee-pee, which is an understandable point, but the Lord does care since we were bought at great price:

> **Flee from sexual immorality. All other sins a person commits are outside the body, but whoever sins sexually, sins against their own body. [19] Do you not know that your bodies are temples of the Holy Spirit, who is in you, whom you have received from God? You are not your own; [20] you were bought at a price. Therefore honor God with your bodies.**
>
> **1 Corinthians 6:18-20**

We are not our own; the LORD purchased us through the precious blood of Christ and we're to offer our bodies as living sacrifices (1 Peter 1:18-19 & Romans 12:1). As far as our thoughts go, the Bible acknowledges that thoughts run our lives and thus God is very interested in what goes on in our minds (Psalm 24:3-5, Proverbs 15:26, Matthew 5:8, Colossians 3:2 & Philippians 4:8). For one, our thought life determines our actions, one way or another.

Personally, I don't masturbate. The Holy Spirit pruned it from me long ago as part of my particular process of sanctification (John 15:1-2). That's my example. How, when, and why the Lord deals with other people on the issue is between them and their Creator. I don't care to know the details because it's a TMI matter of the first order. This doesn't mean, of course, that they can't talk to a spiritual mentor about it if they feel the need to do so, just be sure that he/she is actually *spiritual* and not a gossip (Matthew 7:15-23).

(For instance, I've come across ministers who regularly counsel others and have been known to share details of their counselee by name behind their backs, typically with other ministers. It goes without saying that this is outrageously wrong, but it unfortunately happens).

The reason I decided to cover this topic is because the journey in finding answers from God's Word brings up many issues relevant to one's walk with the Lord in this fallen world, such as spiritual development, self-control, thought life, appreciating beauty vs. lust, walking in the spirit, knowing God, Christianity vs. religious legalism, libertinism, disputable issues and so on.

Our conclusion is that the Liberal view should be dismissed outright because it embraces the folly of libertinism. The Conservative view should be respected and works for many believers while the Middle Ground perspective honestly explores the holes in that view and dares to tackle the ignored details. So the truth lies somewhere between the Conservative position and the Middle Ground position.

Being a decidedly private matter, it's up to each believer to work it out with their Maker on their spiritual journey with fear and trembling.

15

How to Overcome LUST

What good would a book like this be without addressing the problem of lust, which is especially relevant in this day and age? Sexual lust concerns out-of-control preoccupation in deed or thought with porn, fornication, adultery, sexual fantasy, as well as deviant practices, like homosexuality, pedophilia and bestiality.

If you're not a believer in Christ, the first step to freedom from lust is turning to the LORD in repentance & faith (Acts 20:21 & Romans 10:9-10) wherein you'll receive **spiritual regeneration** (John 3:3-6 & Titus 3:5). This means you'll acquire the spiritual hardware necessary to overcome any sin bondage, not to mention the help of the indwelling Spirit.

If you're a believer and you're struggling with sexual lust, you're not alone; many other Christians do too. I did at one time as well. The awesome news is that there's freedom in Christ for everyone in bondage to lust, whatever its form! The sin of lust is similar to any other life-dominating flesh bondage — like alcoholism, out-of-control gambling, drug abuse, greed and hatred — in that the antidote revealed in the Holy Scriptures is the same. The Bible offers a simple **3-point strategy** on how to walk free from any sin, including a severe lust problem, wherein you tackle the issue on three fronts: mental, physical and spiritual.

The solution to being in bondage to the flesh is **spirituality**. That might sound anticlimactic to you, even lame, but let me explain. While 'spirituality' is a term that's thrown around a lot — sometimes by people who aren't really spiritual — it actually refers to the spirit-controlled life. This just means being spirit-driven rather than flesh-ruled; it means being controlled by your higher self as opposed to the lower self. To do this you simply have to learn to put *off* the old self and put *on* the new:

> **You were taught with regard to your former way of life, to put off your old self, which is being corrupted by its deceitful desires; 23 to be made new in the attitude of your minds; 24 and to put on the new self, created to be like God in true righteousness and holiness.**
>
> **Ephesians 4:22-24**

The "old self" is the flesh or sin nature and we are instructed to put it off. Why? Because the old self is corrupted by "deceitful desires." Your flesh has desires, which means it has a voice, but these desires are deceitful. They promise happiness but they don't deliver. They can only ultimately bring death and all that goes with it. We are told to "put off" these fleshly desires. In the Greek this means to strip it off. We have to strip off the old way of thinking in favor of a new way.

Verse 23 tells us how to do this: we must be made new in the attitude of our minds. What's the new attitude we should have? We are to count ourselves dead to the old self and alive to God in Christ Jesus (Romans 6:11). Counting ourselves alive to God includes accepting everything God says we are in Christ, that is, who we are in our new self, the spirit. We'll address this in the next section.

This results in what verse 24 calls "putting on the new self," which refers to a believer living out of his/her spirit as led of the Holy Spirit. When you do this you'll be spirit-controlled and naturally produce the fruit thereof. The New Testament describes this in different ways. When you are spirit-controlled…

- you "live by the spirit" (Galatians 5:16),
- you "clothe yourself with the Lord Jesus Christ" (Romans 13:14),
- you "participate in the divine nature" (2 Peter 1:4), and
- you "put on the new self" (Colossians 3:10).

How can putting on the new self be described as clothing yourself with Christ or participating in the divine nature? Because the "new self" refers to your regenerated spirit, which was "created to be *like God* in true righteousness and holiness" (verse 24).

If there's a *true* righteousness and holiness there's also a *false* righteousness and holiness, which is religious legalism. True righteousness and holiness can only be attained by, first, being born-again spiritually and, second, living out of your spirit rather than the flesh. The latter is a learning process, of course, and takes time, but the more you do it the easier it is and the more fruit you'll produce.

The fruits of the spirit are the fruits of God's nature. Hence, those who live by their spirit, which is guided by the Holy Spirit, will be "like God" because the spirit naturally produces the fruits of God's nature:

> **The acts of the sinful nature are obvious: sexual immorality, impurity and debauchery; [20]idolatry and witchcraft; hatred, discord, jealousy, fits of rage, selfish ambition, dissensions, factions [21] and envy; drunkenness, orgies, and the like. I warn you, as I did before, that those who live like this will not inherit the kingdom of God. [22] But the fruit of the spirit is love, joy, peace, patience, kindness, goodness, faithfulness, [23] gentleness and self-control. Against such things there is no law.**
>
> **Galatians 5:19-23**

This list of the fruit of the spirit isn't exhaustive any more than the list of the works of the flesh is exhaustive. God has many other character traits, like righteousness (Philippians 1:11), truth (Ephesians 5:9), power (2 Timothy 1:7), righteous anger (Mark 3:1-6) and boldness (Mark 11:15-18).

The awesome news is that believers can walk free of the works of the flesh and the two ways they manifest in the Church — legalism and libertinism — simply by putting off the flesh in favor of participating in the divine nature. If this weren't possible Paul would never have instructed us to "be imitators of God" in Ephesians 5:1.

Speaking of Ephesians 5:1, Christians are usually blown away by this verse. They ask, "How can I possibly imitate God?" It's simple: Put off the flesh and learn to live out of your spirit and you'll automatically participate in the divine nature and produce the very fruit of God's character!

So how exactly do you walk in the spirit like this? There are **three things** that you have to do, all corresponding to the three parts of human nature — mind, body and spirit. These are the three keys to walking in the spirit. Let's look at each key, starting with the **mind**.

1. Count Yourself Dead to Sin and Alive to God

The first thing believers need to do in order to walk in the spirit has to do with **the mind**. Paul said that we are to be transformed by the renewing of our mind in Romans 12:2. The Greek word translated as "transformed" is where we get the English 'metamorphosis,' which means to be transformed as the result of a *process*. A great example of this would be a lowly and not-particularly-good-looking caterpillar being transformed in its cocoon and emerging as a beautiful butterfly.

Think about it, caterpillars crawl on the ground and are kind of ugly, whereas butterflies are beautiful and can fly. You can have just as stunning of a transformation, but it involves renewing your mind — you must let go of caterpillar-thinking (flesh-ruled thinking) in favor of butterfly-thinking (spirit-controlled thinking).

Here's a cornerstone passage on renewing the mind and being spirit-controlled:

> **The death he died, he died to sin once for all; but the life he lives, he lives to God.**
> **[11] In the same way, count yourselves dead to sin but alive to God in Christ Jesus. [12] Therefore do not let sin reign in your mortal body so that you obey its evil desires.**
>
> **Romans 6:10-12**

Verse 12 reveals the goal of this instruction — not letting sin reign in your body so that you obey its evil desires. In short, the goal is to *not* be flesh-ruled. Verse 11 shows how to attain this goal: First, you count yourself dead to sin and, second, you count yourself alive to God in Christ Jesus.

Concerning the first part, counting oneself dead to sin involves a new way of thinking. You must start counting yourself as dead to the sins that normally tempt you if you want to experience freedom. For instance, if you have a weakness for lying, gossip, drunkenness or lust, you need to start making it your mindset that you are dead to these things.

I used to have a problem with fits of rage so I had to start making it my mindset that I was dead to fits of rage in order to eventually walk in freedom. Making something your mindset includes making it your confession because words have the power of life and death (Proverbs 18:21). So I made this my regular confession: "I Dirk Waren am dead to fits of rage."

The second part of verse 11 is just as important. You have to count yourself as "alive to God in Christ Jesus." Being alive to God in Christ Jesus is the opposite of being dead to God in the bondage of the flesh. So if you make it your mindset that you're dead to sin, be sure to also make it your mindset that you're alive to the opposite. For example, I made it my belief and confession that I'm dead to fits of rage, but I added that I'm alive to peace and self-control.

Or say if a brother has a problem with lying or exaggerating, he would make it his mindset that he's dead to lying but alive to the truth. Or say if a sister has a problem with gossip and slander (which go hand-and-hand) she would make it her confession that she's dead to gossip/slander and alive to praying for others and blessing them.

Whatever your sin weakness is, count yourself dead to it and counteract it with the truth of *who you already are in your regenerated spirit*. You see, this whole instruction is geared to getting the believer spirit-focused instead of flesh-focused, spirit-controlled instead of flesh-ruled.

For instance, the brother who has a problem with lying has a problem with lying because his flesh has a problem with lying. The only way for him to escape this condition is to stop being flesh-ruled because he'll continue to have a problem with lying as long as he's flesh-ruled. To walk free he'll have to learn to be spirit-controlled by changing his thinking so that it agrees with who he is in his spirit rather than who he is in his flesh.

Remember, your regenerated spirit was "created to be like God in true righteousness and holiness" (Ephesians 4:24). In other words, your spirit is *already* righteous and holy; it doesn't have a sin problem like your lower nature. It's whole and complete, which is what holiness is. The key to freedom is to line up your thinking with who you are in your spirit rather than who you are in your flesh.

This isn't merely a "mind over matter" principle, as some might think. If you're a believer, you can genuinely count yourself dead to sin because you *are* dead to sin in your spirit. Even if you don't feel like you're dead to sin, you *are* dead to sin. It's who you already are in your spirit because *your spirit is righteous and holy like God!*

By the way, renewing your mind in this manner is tied to repentance since 'repent' literally means to change your mind for the better. Both the Greek words for 'repentance' and 'repent' are derived from the Greek word for mind, which is *nous (noos)*. **To repent means to change your thinking, your mindset, your**

attitude, which naturally impacts your actions or lifestyle. Any other type of "repentance" is incomplete and ineffective.

Who Are You "In Him"?

Notice that you are to count yourself alive on to God *in Christ Jesus* (verse 11). Whenever you see phrases like "in Christ" or "in him" in the New Testament they are covenant phraseology. In other words, the passage is stating a fact about the believer who's in covenant with the Lord. Here's an example:

> **God made him who had no sin to be sin for us, so that <u>in him</u> we might become the <u>righteousness of God</u>.**
>
> **2 Corinthians 5:21**

Christ didn't sin, of course, but the Father made him to *be* sin for us on the cross so that all those who enter into covenant with him would become the righteousness of God. The word 'become' in the Greek means to come into being, that is, to be born. Hence, we "become" the righteousness of God through spiritual rebirth. If you're a believer this means that you are already righteous in your spirit and the more spirit-controlled you become the more righteous you will be.

The key to walking in *practical* righteousness is to be spirit-focused rather than flesh-focused because, in your spirit, you already are righteous. With this understanding, as you count yourself dead to sin make sure that you are also counting yourself alive to righteousness. It's the truth because it's who you already are in your spirit. Remember, Jesus said it's the truth that will set you free (John 8:31-32).

There are numerous ways the New Testament describes you in covenant with the LORD. Here are ten:

1. You are **holy** (Colossians 1:21-22).
2. You are a **child of God** (John 1:12-13).
3. You are a **new creation** (2 Corinthians 5:17).
4. You are the **righteousness of God** (2 Corinthians 5:21).
5. You are **dead to sin** (Romans 6:11,14,18).
6. You are **more than a conqueror** (Romans 8:37).
7. You are a **temple of the Holy Spirit** (1 Corinthians 6:19-20).
8. You are **rich** (2 Corinthians 8:9).
9. You are **healed** (1 Peter 2:24).
10. You are a **royal priest** or **priestess** of the Most High God (1 Peter 2:9).

These are all "positional truths." A positional truth is any truth from the Scriptures that reveals your *position* in covenant with the LORD and therefore *how God sees you* because of this position. For instance, Colossians 1:22 declares that we are "holy **in His sight**, without blemish and free from accusation." This is **how God sees you** because this is ***who you are*** in Christ.

Just be wise to 'fess up when you miss it so that God can faithfully purify you from all unrighteousness (1 John 1:8-9). This is "keeping with repentance" (Matthew & Luke 3:8). Don't allow the build-up of unconfessed sin to block the power and favor of God in your life. A side benefit of this is that it keeps your heart soft and malleable rather than hard and incorrigible.

For the New Testament believer, meaning YOU, these ten descriptions reveal ***who you are*** in your spirit, the "new self" (Ephesians 4:22-24).

How do you practice such positional truths? You practice them simply by believing them and not disagreeing with them. Remember, "The tongue has the power of life and death" so utilize this power accordingly. Never speak words that contradict who God says you are. Never! This is tantamount to calling God a liar.

Be sure to chew on these amazing positional truths and others as well. Make them your meditation and your confession. Take David, for example. He was diligent to "meditate" on God's Word, as shown in Psalm 119:15-16. The Hebrew word for 'meditate' is *siach (SEE-akh)*, which means "to ponder and converse with oneself and, hence, out loud." As you do this with these positional truths, you'll grow in understanding and power. The more these truths become a part of you, the more you'll be set free of the flesh and the more you'll soar in the spirit free of the limitations of the fleshly plane.

The Lord said in John 8:31-32 that we must "continue" in his word if we are to "know the truth" and be set "free." Unlike your spiritual rebirth which happened instantaneously, your metamorphosis from caterpillar-thinking to butterfly-thinking is a *process*; it may not happen overnight, but it will happen, so don't give up. If you miss it, be quick to repent and God will forgive you, and then keep moving forward. You don't drown by falling in the water; you drown by staying in the water![9]

If all you do is change your thinking to focus on who you already are in your spirit — dead to sin, righteous, holy — you'll be blessed and walk in more freedom than ever. But there are two other keys to participating in the divine nature and they have to do with your **body** and your **spirit**.

---

[9] For more on how to practice positional truth see my video *How God Sees YOU* at the FOL site (also available on Youtube).

2. Offering Your Body as a Living Sacrifice

Let's go back to Romans 6:11-12 and see what it goes on to say:

> **In the same way, count yourselves dead to sin but alive to God in Christ Jesus. [12] Therefore do not let sin reign in your mortal body so that you obey its evil desires. [13] Do not offer the parts of your body to sin, as instruments of wickedness, but rather offer yourselves to God, as those who have been brought from death to life; and offer the parts of your body to him as instruments of righteousness. [14] For sin shall not be your master, because you are not under law, but under grace.**
>
> **Romans 6:11-14**

Since believers are dead to sin and alive to God in our spirits, Paul says that we shouldn't offer the parts of our bodies to sin as instruments of wickedness, but rather to God as instruments of righteousness. We can do this because we've been brought from a condition of spiritual death to spiritual life, as verse 13 points out.

All unbelievers are spiritually dead. This doesn't mean they don't have a spirit and the capacity for good, but rather that their spirit is dead to God, which means that the ability to commune with the LORD doesn't exist. They're cut off from a relationship with their Creator because their spirit *can't* connect or commune with God.

Yet it's precisely because they have a spirit that they desperately want to connect with the Creator, even though it's impossible (Mark 10:26-27). This, of course, gives birth to religion, which is **the human attempt to connect with God**. Authentic Christianity, by contrast, is **God connecting with us** through spiritual rebirth in Christ by the Holy Spirit.

In this passage from Romans Paul reasons that, since we've been brought from a condition of spiritual death to spiritual life, we are to offer **the parts of our bodies** to God's service as instruments of righteousness. This refers to two things:

1. Put into practice the truths you discover in Scripture, whether from your own studies or through receiving from others. In other words, line up your body with what God's Word teaches. This doesn't just include practical truths like "Husbands love your wives, just as Christ loved the church and gave himself up for her," but positional truths as well. How so? Because it takes your brain and your tongue to practice positional truth and both are parts of your body. If your brain and tongue aren't lining up with what God's Word says about you then you're not offering these parts of your body to the LORD as instruments of righteousness.
2. Put into practice whatever instruction God gives you, which includes serving in any role you're called to perform or moving toward any objective he gives you. Seek the Lord in prayer concerning your purpose, both short-range and long-range. What are you inspired to do for God? What area of service really stirs you? Colossians 3:15 says to "let the peace of Christ rule in your hearts." What do you have a peace about doing? In other words, what do you have a good feeling about? Identify your strengths and then major in them. Grasp the unique task God has called you to do in each season of your life. Whatever it is, start doing it and

> ask for God's strength and direction. A journey of a thousand miles starts with the first step.[10]

When you begin utilizing the parts of your body as instruments of righteousness in God's service the law of displacement comes into play. Light displaces darkness; righteousness displaces wickedness; spirit replaces flesh. Sin shall *not* be your master for you are not under law (legalism) but under grace (spirituality)!

A Living Sacrifice in Worship

There's even more to offering yourself to God:

> **Therefore, I urge you, brothers and sisters, in view of God's mercy, to offer your bodies as living sacrifices, holy and pleasing to God—this is your spiritual act of worship. [2] Do not conform any longer to the pattern of this world, but be transformed by the renewing of your mind. Then you will be able to test and approve what God's will is—his good, pleasing and perfect will.**
>
> **Romans 12:1-2**

This passage plainly details the first two steps to spirituality; that is, being spirit-controlled. Verse 2 instructs us to be transformed by the renewing of our minds, which we've already addressed, while verse 1 tells us to offer our bodies to God as "living sacrifices" and adds "this is your spiritual act of *worship*." 'Worship' means to "reverently honor or adore."

---

[10] For a scriptural **3-point plan of action** see the article *How to Obtain Your Desires* at the FOL site (and the corresponding video).

You can worship in two ways: Through your **actions** and through your **communion**:

1. Actions have to do with *practice.* When you sincerely practice the truths of God's Word you are also honoring the LORD, which is worship. It's the same thing when you start lining-up your life with God's particular assignment for you, big or small, you're worshipping the Creator. Either way, your actions give glory to God.
2. Communion, however, has to do with *communication.* Prayer is communion with God and you specifically honor the LORD through the type of prayer known as praise & worship.

What exactly is praise & worship? The two go hand-and-hand. Praise is celebration and includes thanksgiving, raving and boasting; whereas worship is adoration. Praise naturally attracts God's presence and is in accordance with the law of respect: What you respect moves toward you whereas what you don't respect moves away from you. Worship, on the other hand, is adoration or awe, and is the response to being in the LORD's presence. See Psalm 95:1-7 and Psalm 100 for verification.

You'll see this principle at work in relationships all the time. Take, for instance, romantic relationships. Say if a woman is interested in a man and she praises his work, how will this make him feel? He'll feel important and respected. He'll feel like the "king of the world" and will naturally be more inclined to the woman, even if she's someone he might not have noticed otherwise. It's the same principle with God. When you start praising the Lord and boasting of your Creator, God'll naturally be more inclined toward you. It's a simple principle.

We can further differentiate praise & worship as such:

- Praise celebrates God whereas worship humbly reveres God.
- Praise lifts the Lord up while worship bows when the Lord is lifted.
- Praise dances before God whereas worship pulls off God's shoes.
- Praise extols the Lord for what he's done while worship adores the Lord for who he is.
- Praise says "Praise the Lord" whereas worship demonstrates that he is Lord.
- Praise is thanksgiving for being a co-heir in Christ while worship lays the crown at the Lord's feet.

Many believers are more comfortable with worshipping God through what they do rather than through communion, but I encourage you to excel in both. I run across a lot of wives who complain that their husbands rarely tell them that they love them, if ever. They hardly even compliment them. When confronted, the husband typically argues that he loves his wife by doing things for her, including working hard to bring home the bread. This is wonderful, of course, but the wife *still* wants to hear him communicate it to her. Do you think it's any different with God?

Some men tend to veer away from praise & worship because they think it's girly somehow. But, let me tell you something, David is one of the most passionate praise & worship warriors recorded in the Bible and he was wholly masculine. As a teenager he had the great faith and boldness to challenge the hulking Goliath with a slingshot when the entire army of Israel was shrinking back in terror (1 Samuel 17:24)! He went on to become one of the greatest kings of Israel, but God wouldn't allow him to build the temple because he was a warrior king and had too much blood on his hands! See 1 Chronicles 28:3. Does this sound like a girly man?

Or consider Moses' aide, Joshua. After Moses spoke with God in the Tent of Meeting, Joshua would stay and linger in God's presence (Exodus 33:11). Guess who God later chose to lead the Israelites in the conquest of Canaan? Joshua. There's clearly a link between those who choose to be mighty praise & worship warriors for God and those who are mighty warriors in God's service. Those who are "ever praising" the LORD and who dwell in God's presence "go from strength to strength" (Psalm 84:4-7). They are "transformed into his likeness with ever-increasing glory, which comes from the Lord, who is the Spirit" (2 Corinthians 3:18). In light of all this, anyone who claims that praise & worship is worthless or sissified is grossly ignorant.

Needless to say, every believer is called to deeper praise & worship. It will literally revolutionize your life, as it has mine and continues to do so.

If all you did was practice these first two keys to being spirit-controlled you'll be greatly blessed and experience freedom to a higher degree than ever. But there's one more step and it has to do with your **spirit**. It's what the Bible calls praying in the spirit.

3. Praying in the Spirit and Charging Yourself Up

Let's look at a couple of key passages about praying in the spirit:

> **But you, dear friends, <u>build yourselves up</u> in your most holy faith and <u>pray in the Holy Spirit</u>.**
>
> **Jude 1:20**

This verse shows that believers in general should "build themselves up" in faith by praying in the Holy Spirit. It gives the impression of charging up one's faith like a battery. In the Greek "build yourselves up" means "to build upon." You see, every believer has a measure of faith at the time of salvation (Romans 12:3), but this measure can be built upon as the believer grows.

In other words, believers *should* increase in faith as they mature. How do you do this? One way is through God's Word (Romans 10:17), another is by spending time in God's presence through praise & worship; after all, the LORD is full of faith and therefore those who hang around God will develop the same faith. It's the law of association.

Jude 1:20 (above) shows that praying in the Spirit is also essential for increasing in faith. Here's another passage on praying in the spirit:

> **And pray in the Spirit on all occasions with all kinds of prayers and requests.**
>
> **Ephesians 6:18**

This verse appears right after Paul details the six pieces of the "armor of God," which shows that praying in the spirit is actually the seventh piece of the armor even though he doesn't analogize it like he does with the other six pieces (e.g. faith is a "shield" and the Word of God is a "sword"). I liken praying in the spirit to *artillery* or a *missile* since you can pray in the spirit for people and situations a long distance away, even on the other side of the planet.

So we're clearly instructed in the Scriptures to charge our faith up by praying in the spirit and also to pray in the spirit on all occasions with all kinds of prayers and requests. The question now is, what is "praying in the Spirit"? After all, one can't very well pray in the spirit if you don't even know what it is. Thankfully, the Bible tells us exactly what it is:

> **For if I pray in a tongue, my spirit prays, but my mind is unfruitful. [15] So what shall I do? I will pray with my spirit, but I will also pray with my mind; I will sing with my spirit, but I will also sing with my mind.**
>
> **1 Corinthians 14:14-15**

By saying "if I pray in a tongue, my spirit prays" Paul was defining praying in the spirit: If he prayed in a tongue his spirit was praying, led of the Holy Spirit, and therefore he was praying in the spirit or praying in the Spirit (capitalized).[11]

Praying in the spirit is synonymous with speaking in tongues, which is also known as glossolalia *(gloss-ah-LAY-lee-ah)*. What is speaking in tongues? It's when a believer prays from his spirit rather than his mind and therefore speaks in a language unknown to him. We see this in verse 15 where Paul notes two types of prayer — praying with his spirit and praying with his mind, singing with his spirit and singing with his mind.

Praying with your mind is obvious, it's praying with a language you understand, which is typically the language you most often speak. For me it would be English. When I pray in English I'm praying with my mind because it's a language I know and understand. Praying with one's mind is wonderful and this is usually what people think of when they think of prayer. Yet when you pray in this manner you are limited to your own understanding. Whatever it is you're praying for — whether a

---

[11] Since there is no capitalization in the original Greek text, translators have to determine if the word for spirit, *pneuma*, refers to the human spirit (un-capitalized) or the Holy Spirit (capitalized). Either/or works in this case since the human spirit prays by the Holy Spirit due to the fact that the believer's human spirit (un-capitalized) is rebirthed and indwelt by the Spirit (capitalized). See John 3:6, Ephesians 3:16, 1 Corinthians 6:17 and Romans 8:10 & 8:16.

person, place or situation — you're limited to your own understanding.

This is where praying in the spirit comes into play. Praying in the spirit, aka speaking in tongues, bypasses the limitations of one's understanding as led of the Holy Spirit. For instance, say if I'm praying for a believer who's struggling with a certain sin and has backslid to some degree. If I pray with my mind — my understanding — I am limited to what I know about the situation, but if I pray in the spirit for him I can address things beyond my understanding as led of the Holy Spirit.

Or say if you're going to lose your job due to budget cuts or whatever in six months, but you of course don't know it's going to happen. You can't pray about it with your mind since you don't even know it's going to occur.

Thankfully, the Holy Spirit knows everything because the Spirit is God and indwells your spirit (Ephesians 3:16 & Romans 8:16), not to mention guides you (John 16:13). So when you pray in the spirit the Holy Spirit will likely guide your spirit to pray for your encouragement and a new job opportunity when you lose your current one in six months. You may not know about it yet, but the Holy Spirit does. As such, you were able to address something in prayer that your mind didn't even know about through praying in the spirit. You bypassed the limitations of your understanding.

This is why Paul encouraged us to "pray in the Spirit on all occasions" in Ephesians 6:18 and it's why he stressed that he would pray and sing with both his mind and his spirit. *Both* are important.

The gift of personal tongues is for *all believers,* which is why these passages on praying in the spirit refer to all believers and not just to some who have a special gift. Note how none of these passages say anything like "Now, *if* you have the gift of tongues, pray in the spirit on all occasions" or "*If* you can speak in tongues build yourself up in faith by praying in the Holy Spirit." Back when these passages were written it was assumed that all believers had the gift of personal tongues. Virtually every believer had it because leaders in the church didn't shy away from emphasizing the importance of the baptism of the Holy Spirit, as they do today, unfortunately.

I describe praying in the spirit as "personal tongues" to distinguish it from the gift of tongues utilized in a church service, which is followed by an interpretation in the common language. A tongue *plus* an interpretation is equal to a prophecy just like two nickels equal a dime. Not everyone has *this* gift, which Paul made clear in 1 Corinthians 12:30.

The kind of speaking in tongues we're discussing here is different and refers to the believer praying *to God* with his/her spirit as led of the Holy Spirit. This is for *all* believers. Public tongues, on the other hand, isn't actually praying in the spirit because the believer who is operating in this gift isn't praying *to God*, but is rather giving a message *from God* to the believers present for their exhortation and encouragement.

One refers to the believer praying to God with his/her spirit and the other refers to God speaking to the congregation via a tongue, which requires an interpretation; and this makes it prophesying. One is a form of prayer and the other is a form of prophesying. They're quite different. All believers can have the gift of personal tongues, but not all believers have the gift of public tongues. It's important to distinguish the two.

If every believer can have the gift of personal tongues and you don't yet have it, how do you receive it? See the article at the FOL site *Baptism of the Holy Spirit and Its Benefits*.

Recapping the Three Keys to Walking in the Spirit

So the three keys to being spirit-controlled rather than flesh-ruled are as follows:

1. **Renew your mind.** Make it your mindset that you are dead to sin but alive to God in Christ Jesus. This includes making it your confession. Say: "I [state your name] am dead to sin and alive to God in Christ Jesus." Renewing your mind effectively includes lining up your thoughts and words with who God's Word says you already are in Christ. For instance, the Bible says that you're dead to sin, holy, righteous and more than a conqueror in covenant with the Lord. These all describe who you are in your spirit as opposed to the flesh. You may not feel like you are these things, but you *already are* in your spirit. By accepting these positional truths by faith you're being spirit-focused rather than flesh-focused. Do it.
2. **Offer the parts of your body to God as instruments of righteousness.** This includes serving the Lord — doing what God wants you to do (both general instructions from the Scriptures and specific instructions from the Spirit) — but also praise & worship. Each of these puts into motion the law of displacement. By moving forward in the spirit you aren't slipping backwards in the flesh. By spending time in the light of God's presence through regular praise & worship darkness has no recourse but to flee. How do you get the darkness out of a room? You simple turn on the lights!

3. **Pray (and sing) in the spirit regularly.** This will keep you charged up and built-up in faith. It'll produce the power you need to walk in the full life Christ came to give us (John 10:10). It'll empower you to *agape* love people you don't have warm feelings toward, including your enemies who hate you without cause. It'll enable you to walk in *tough* love when necessary, including righteous radicalness, like when Paul rebuked an arrogant sorcerer and temporarily cursed him with blindness to humble him, as led of the Holy Spirit (Acts 13:8-12). It'll provide the self-discipline necessary to overcome personal weaknesses, including lack of confidence, depression and various sin problems, like alcoholism, drugs, lying, gossip/slander and sexual lust.

Practicing these three principles is simply a matter of wisdom and love. The first and greatest command is to love God with all your heart and the second is to love people as you love yourself (Matthew 22:34-39). This is the New Covenant law of Christ or law of love (Galatians 6:2 & 1 Corinthians 9:21), which is different from the Mosaic law that believers are *not* under (Romans 7:6 & Galatians 5:18).

In a sense there are three commands in the law of Christ since we are commanded to **love God** and **love others** *as* we **love ourselves**, which means you have to love yourself first. I mean that in a healthy sense, of course, and not a narcissistic one. If you genuinely love yourself you'll put these principles into practice on a regular basis. After all, if you fail to implement them you won't have a victorious Christian life and you won't be intimate with God. You'll be encumbered and limited by personal weaknesses or areas of the flesh. This will not bless you, it won't bless those linked to you, and it won't bless God.

Practicing these three principles is the key to walking in the spirit or participating in the divine nature. It's the key to producing the fruit of the spirit and, therefore, being *spiritual* rather than *carnal*. Simply put, it's the key to being spirit-controlled rather than flesh-ruled. The former gives life while the latter brings death.

24/7 "God-Consciousness"

This is the key to having a vital, active relationship with God, which is the antidote to all forms of sin, whether legalistic in nature or libertine. By "active relationship" I don't mean thinking about God once or twice a day, but rather 24/7 God-consciousness in which you're **in constant connection and communion**. This makes sense of Paul's instruction to "pray without ceasing" in 1 Thessalonians 5:17 (KJV). How can anyone possibly "pray without ceasing"? By participating in the divine nature and walking in 24/7 God-consciousness.

A close relationship with your heavenly Father by the Spirit thru Jesus Christ requires the same time and attention that any close relationship requires. Like those relationships, it's not a chore, but a joy and an honor. It develops over time. David said, "Taste and see that the LORD is good" (Psalm 34:8). Once you've genuinely tasted of a relationship with God nothing else in life compares. It's the ultimate high!

It's your choice. You've been granted the awesome power of DECISION, which is volition. Whether you know it or not, you operated in this power to receive eternal salvation (Romans 10:9-10). Use this God-given gift to your advantage in your Christian walk. You're not a loser, you're a winner. Go forth and walk in the freedom and victory that God has bought for you at great cost!

Rise up O man of God, rise up O woman of God, and soar on the heights in the spirit far above the limitations of the mental realm and the flesh! Amen.

"Put Off the Old Man"

One last exhortation before closing: It's imperative that you put off the "old man" — the flesh — in order for this to work. This is the very first thing we are instructed to do in Ephesians 4:22-24. We see the same instruction in this passage:

> **Do not lie to one another, since you have put off the old man with his deeds, [10] and have put on the new man who is renewed in knowledge according to the image of Him who created him,**
>
> **Colossians 3:9-10** (NKJV)

Before you can put on the new man — that is, effectively walk in the spirit — you have to be willing to put off the old man and "his" fleshly deeds. This means repenting of any area of the flesh once it is revealed to you as sin. You see, God deals with his children according to the light we have. Once we have revelation of something we are responsible for living according to it. See John 9:39-41 and 15:22 for verification. And, no, this isn't an excuse to stay in ignorance.

Let me give a widespread example. In Westernized cultures today fornication is viewed as a normal lifestyle, but it's a sin according to God's Word. When the average male turns to the Lord he'll often come into the kingdom with the attitude that there's nothing wrong with fornication since it's such a prominent activity. Besides, "everyone does it," he might reason. As he grows spiritually, however, he comes to realize that it's wrong and God has something better for him. Up until this point God would automatically overlook transgressions in this area because he was corrupted by worldly culture and just didn't know any better. Once he *knows* the truth, however, he's obligated to walk according to it.

This is simply a matter of loving God, which is the first and greatest command (1 John 2:15-17). It's also a matter of wisdom or common sense. Yet I'm surprised at how many people refuse to give up fornication after becoming believers and discovering it's a sin. Then they wonder why they don't feel close to the LORD and they're not blessed. I'll tell you why, they're not putting off the old man! They're being stubborn and foolish.

Think about it like this: Say you're a parent and have a baby who soiled her diaper. You take the old diaper off, clean her up, and then put on the new diaper. Wouldn't it be absurd to put the new diaper over the old diaper? Yet this is what many Christians do in effect when they refuse to put off the old man before putting on the new. They try to put the new man over the old man and it doesn't work. No wonder they're frustrated!

So please be sure to put off the deceitful desires of the flesh by **keeping in repentance** (Matthew & Luke 3:8).

Repentance *and* Faith

We saw earlier that repent simply means to change one's mind for the positive. This doesn't mean a meaningless mental exercise, but rather a change of mind with **the corresponding actions**, like the resolve to fulfill God's will (Acts 26:20) and turn from that which is opposed to God's will, i.e. sin (Acts 8:22 & 2 Corinthians 12:21).

Repentance and faith are two sides of the same coin, as verified by Mark 1:15 and Acts 20:21. So for repentance to be effective **it must be combined with faith**, otherwise repentance is just a dead exercise. Is it any wonder that repentance and faith are the first two doctrines of the six basic doctrines of Christianity? See Hebrews 6:1-2. It is of the utmost importance to your spiritual health to grasp this.

Epilogue

I trust you have a better understanding of the amazing Song of Songs, as well as fresh scriptural insights on art, love, marriage and sex, not to mention overcoming lust and the flesh in general. Let's close with the relevant question…

Will People Marry and Have Sex in Eternity?

Christ said "At the resurrection **people will neither marry nor be given in marriage**; they will be *like* the angels in heaven" (Matthew 22:30). He didn't say people would *be* angels, just that — like angels — we won't marry or be given in marriage (not to mention we'll be immortal like angels, if you compare the verse with the fuller account in Luke 20:34-36).[12]

A possible reason there will be no marriage is that in the eternal age of the New Heavens and New Earth (2 Peter 3:13 & Revelation 21:1-4) we will experience the transparency and intimacy with the Lord that many of us enjoy now with our spouses, albeit to the nth degree. Keep in mind that the Church is

[12] As far as immortality goes, see 2 Timothy 1:10, Romans 2:7 and John 3:36.

called the "bride of Christ" and thus we will in essence be **married to the Lord in eternity** (2 Corinthians 11:2 & Revelation 19:7-9).

Furthermore, since the redeemed are collectively the "bride," it suggests transparency and closeness with *all* fellow redeemed people.

Think about it, what separates us from other people, including fellow believers? What keeps us all from being close? What keeps us from being honest and transparent with each other? Answer: Either **1.** issues of the flesh, i.e. sin, or **2.** because of lies and error. For instance, you might have to separate from Christians because they're impenitent gossips/slanderers and the Bible instructs us to not even eat with such people (1 Corinthians 5:11). Or someone believes lies about you and thus refuses to associate with you. Or the assembly down the street embraces grossly false doctrines, which naturally hinders fellowship with them.

Thankfully, sin, lies and error will no longer exist in the eternal New Heavens and New Earth (Revelation 21:7-8,26-27). Since these maladies will no longer hinder relationships and keep us apart, there will be true unity, closeness, honesty and harmony. Praise God!

A secondary reason for the absence of marriage in the eternal age-to-come might be that God doesn't want humans propagating any further since there will be more than enough for his purposes in the New Heavens and New Earth.

May the LORD bless you in your service as you continually draw closer to God, seek the truth, and apply what you've learned.

Amen.

Appendix

Proposed Outlines of the Love Triangle Interpretation

For your convenience, I'd like to share a couple of general outlines of the three-character interpretation, neither of which are set-in-stone (in other words, they can be tweaked):

I. The Shulammite maiden is separated from her shepherd lover by the king of Israel and taken into his regal tents (1:1-11).

- **A.** Yet she can't help but soliloquize over her shepherd lover (1:1-4).
- **B.** She responds to the city women of the court who seem contemptuous (1:5-6).
- **C.** She soliloquizes more concerning her beloved shepherd (1:7).
- **D.** The ladies reply (1:8).
- **E.** King Solomon's voices his esteem for the Shulammite maiden (1:9-11).

II. The Shulammite and her shepherd lover together, possibly a remembered exchange or daydream (1:12-2:6).

- **A.** She speaks (1:12-14).
- **B.** He speaks (1:15).
- **C.** She speaks (1:16-2:1).
- **D.** He speaks (2:2).
- **E.** She speaks (2:3-6).

III. Disconnected from her beloved shepherd and in the imperial tents she informs the women of the court of her lover (2:7-3:5).

- **A.** She tells them not to arouse love for anyone until it's the right time (2:7).
- **B.** She informs them of her initial meeting with her beloved shepherd (2:8-14).
- **C.** She is delayed by her brothers who send her out to work in their family's vineyard (2:15).
- **D.** She relates how she waited for her betrothed to return in the later hours (2:16-17).
- **E.** She details her quest for her beloved and how she queried the guards (3:1-3).
- **F.** She conveys how she discovers him (3:4).

IV. The maiden and her lover reunited (3:6-5:1).

- **A.** The citizens of Jerusalem observe King Solomon's oncoming procession and remark (3:6-11).
- **B.** The shepherd has followed the procession from Shunem and enters Jerusalem. (4:1-5).
  - **1.** He acquires a meeting and again praises her.
  - **2.** (Compare the shepherd's noble decorum with the king's adulations detailed in 6:4-10 and 7:1-9).
- **C.** The Shulammite maiden offers to come back, speaking of 2:17 (4:6).
- **D.** Bolstered by her loveliness and faithfulness, the shepherd offers his succor (4:7-15).
- **E.** She proclaims that all she has is to please him (4:16).

- **F.** He answers that he is coming (5:1).

V. The Shulammite maiden and her shepherd lover separate (5:2-8:4).

- **A.** Her dialogues with the women of the court (5:2-6:3).
  - **1.** She shares a dream she had about her shepherd lover (5:2-8).
  - **2.** Amazed, the women ask what distinguishes him above other men (5:9).
  - **3.** She details his attributes (5:10-16).
  - **4.** They desire to witness such a man and ask where to find him (6:1).
  - **5.** Suspicious, she evades their inquiries (6:2-3).
- **B.** Her dialogues with the king of Israel (6:4-8:4).
  - **1.** Solomon's flatteries (6:4-10).
  - **2.** She clarifies that her encounter with him was not deliberate (6:11-12).
  - **3.** She seeks to go back home so Solomon renews his flatteries (6:13-7:9).
  - **4.** She rejects the king and asks her shepherd lover to take her back to Shunem (7:10-8:4).
    - **a.** She charges the court ladies once again concerning true love (8:4).

VI. The Shulammite returns to her pastoral home with her shepherd lover (8:5-14).

- **A.** Friends of the shepherd see them coming (8:5a).
- **B.** The two lovers return to the locale where they pledged their fidelity and renew their vows (8:5b-7).
- **C.** Her brothers deliberate about her dowry (8:8-12).
  - **1.** Is she a "wall" (honorable) or "door" (loose)? (8:8-9).
  - **2.** "I am a wall not a door" (8:10-12).
- **D.** The shepherd requests that she tell the story (8:13).
- **E.** She possesses the shepherd as her beloved (8:14).
  - **1.** He is to rush to her now and for life.

2. No more mountains to separate them (2:8,17).
3. These have given way to the mountains of delight (8:14).

Here's a simpler variation:

I. Although in the king's "chambers," the Shulammite voices her love for her betrothed shepherd (1:2-4).

II. Solomon praises the maiden's beauty while she amusingly extols her fiancé's virtues (1:8-3:4).
   - A. Longing for her betrothed, she reminisces of their past days together.
   - B. As well as dreams of seeing him again.

III. Possibly an account of when Solomon met the Shulammite lass (3:6-11).

IV. The humble bridegroom describes his fiancée's beauty (4:1-15).
   - A. She responds (4:16).

V. The Shulammite dreams of reuniting with her beloved (5:2-7).
   - A. It morphs into a nightmare.

VI. She explains to the ladies from the city what's so special about her betrothed shepherd (5:10-16).

VII. The king once again flatters her (6:4-9).
   - A. He graphically expresses his carnal desire for her (7:1-9).
   - B. Yet he is an intruder upon the heart of one who belongs to another (7:10).

VIII. Fiancée and fiancé are reunited and journey back to their rural village up north (7:11-8:7).
   - A. The country girl's devotion to her lowly shepherd enabled her to resist the king's advances.
   - B. Her love for him could not be swayed or weakened despite the allure of Solomon's pomp and riches.

C. The king promised her an expensive vineyard to join his marriage club,[13] but she was content (8:11-12).

Remember, these are merely *proposed* outlines, the first being loosely based on Dake's take and the second derived from David Kirkwood's commentaries. I included both to show that there's a considerable range of interpretation even within the same basic view.

Needless to say, these outlines should not be regarded as rigid interpretations that you *must* follow. Use your God-given imagination and consider possible alterations.

Also remember that the Song of Songs is a work of art and therefore it's up to the one reading the lyrics to interpret it, glean from it, and relate the morals of the story to his/her life, hopefully with the help of the Holy Spirit.

Personally, I've never read the Song of Songs with a rigid outline in mind. I appreciate it as a work of art that just so happens to be God-breathed Scripture; and glean from it thereof.

---

[13] It was noted in chapter **2** that Solomon ultimately acquired 700 wives, not to mention 300 concubines (1 Kings 11:3). I suppose you could call the wives *The 700 Club*.

Bibliography

Anderson, Don. *Song of Solomon: Make Full My Joy.* Neptune: Loizeaux Brothers, 1987

Brown, Francis/Driver, S.R./Briggs, Charles A. *Brown-Driver-Briggs Lexicon.* Peabody: Hendrickson Publishers, 1994

Bullinger, Ethelbert W. *A Critical Lexicon and Concordance to the English and Greek New Testament.* Grand Rapids: Zondervan Publishing House, 1975

Conrad, Joseph. *Heart of Darkness and The Secret Sharer.* New York: Bantam Books, 1902/1987

Dake, Finis. *Dake's Annotated Reference Bible.* Lawrenceville: DBS, 1963/1991

Helps Word-Studies Lexicon. Retrieved from Biblehub.com. 1987, 2011

Kirkwood, David. *Your Best Year Yet!* Pittsburgh: Ethnos Press, 1996

LORD, The. *The Amplified Bible.* Grand Rapids: Zondervan, 1987

LORD, The. *English Standard Version (ESV). Holy Bible*. Chicago: Crossway, 2001

LORD, The. *The International Standard Version New Testament.* Highlands Ranch: Davidson Press, 1998

LORD, The. *King James Version. Holy Bible.* Iowa Falls: World Bible Publishers

LORD, The. *New International Version (Revised). Holy Bible.* Nashville: Holman, 2011

LORD, The. *New King James Version Study Bible: Second Edition. Holy Bible.* Nashville: Thomas Nelson, 2012

LORD, *The. New Revised Standard Version. Holy Bible.* Nashville: Nelson, 1989

LORD, The. *Quest Study Bible: New International Version. Holy Bible.* Grand Rapids: Zondervan, 2003

MacArthur, John. *The MacArthur Study Bible.* Nashville: Word Bibles, 1997

Roberts, Patti. *Ashes to Gold.* Word Publishing, 1985

Strong, James. *Strong's Exhaustive Concordance.* Grand Rapids: Baker, 1991

Various authors. *The New Oxford Annotated Apocrypha: New Revised Standard Version.* Oxford University Press, 2018

Vine, W.E. *Vine's Expository Dictionary of Biblical Words.* Cambridge: Nelson, 1985

Waren, Dirk. *The Four Stages of Spiritual Growth.* Youngstown: Soaring Eagle Press, 2015

Waren, Dirk. *Legalism Unmasked.* Youngstown: Soaring Eagle Press, 2013/2018

Waren, Dirk. *Women in Ministry ...in God's Service.* Youngstown: Soaring Eagle Press, 2021

Fountain of Life

Teaching Ministry

(Psalm 36:9)

The mission of Fountain of Life is to **set the captives FREE** by **reaching the world** with the **life-changing truths of God's Word**, the **power of the Holy Spirit** and the **Awesome News of the message of Jesus Christ**.

We're calling Spiritual Warriors all over the Earth to partner with us on this mission!

Books by Dirk Waren:

The Believer's Guide to FORGIVENESS & WARFARE
Legalism Unmasked
HELL KNOW! (full and condensed versions)
SHEOL KNOW! (full and condensed versions)
The Four Stages of Spiritual Growth
ANGELS: Their Purpose and Your Responsibility
THE LAW and the Believer
The SIX BASIC DOCTRINES of Christianity
GRACE: What is It? How Do You Grow in It?
How to Handle OFFENSES: Personal & Criminal
WOMEN in Ministry ...in God's Service
The FIVEFOLD MINISTRY Gifts: Apostle, Prophet, Evangelist, Pastor, Teacher
Solomon's SONG OF SONGS and Issues of Love & Sex

www.ingramcontent.com/pod-product-compliance
Lightning Source LLC
LaVergne TN
LVHW050547160826
845677LV00011B/2219

9798218041571